MILLENNIUM

Hakim Bey

١٢٢١

◆ **MILLENNIUM** ◆
Hakim Bey

Autonomedia
&
Garden of Delight

Anti-Copyright @1996
May be freely copied and distributed, but please
query the author and publisher about translations.

Autonomedia
POB 568
Williamsburgh Station
Brooklyn, New York
11211-0568 USA

Garden of Delight
Publications
3 Castle Street
Dublin 2,
Ireland

Phone & Fax: 718-963-2603
EMail: semiotexte@aol.com

Phone:01.475.0075
EMail: Glendale@indigo.IE

Printed in the United States of America

Contents

Interview with Hakim Bey 7
Millennium 29
For and Against Interpretation 57
Religion and Revolution 69
Note on Nationalism 87

Interview with Hakim Bey

[A longer version appears as preface to the German translation of *Immediatism*]

10 July, 1996
New York — Vienna
(by phone)

Q: [The first questions concern the book *Immediatism* (a.k.a. *Radio Sermonettes*) and readers' response to it]:

A: Of course it's meant as a discussion of what people do rather than what people *should* do. I'm really not interested in preaching, and I don't think myself a guru in any sense. More than that, in this particular book I really meant to describe what I considered to be the revolutionary potential of everyday life, to put it in Situationist terms. The response has been pretty good — I mean I don't get hundreds of letters or anything, but I do get lots of letters, and I do get lots of response — and it seems to strike a chord especially with people in the arts, which is who it was meant for really. I mean, when I say people in the arts that could be anybody, not just professional artists; it could be anyone who feels a necessity for creative action in their life. My idea was to define a space which I feel exists (anyway), that's a private, even secret space, if you like...clandestine...in which the whole problem of commodification, the buying and selling of art, the turning of art into a commodity and the use of art to sell commodities, which is sort of a curse for the modern artist, is avoided, just plain avoided; just a withdrawal from that world and a reaffirmation of a creative power in everyday life, outside the life of commodity, the life of the market. After all, this is why all artists are artists, this is why one becomes an artist — not to sell your soul to the company store but to create.

Q: Is there a lot of media interest in what you do? — because somehow the Disappearing One could attract lots of attention, and the one who places a critique could become himself very interesting for the media. How would that circle work for you?

A: You're absolutely right, but it has not really worked that way. It's true that TAZ ["The Temporary Autonomous Zone"] was part of a book which caused a little bit of a stir in underground circles or whatever, there was some publicity involved in this, but in the first place I don't seek publicity for myself — I'm not interested in establishing some sort of personality cult. I really would like to be invisible. Actually, it was probably a mistake to use an exotic name to write this material. It does actually draw curiosity and attention instead of just being accepted as a pseudonym. So there was a little bit of media attention but not very much, and one reason for that is that in America nothing reaches the media unless it's commodification. This is all the media is interested in, something which can sell products. And there's no product to be sold here other than a small cheap book or two. In Europe things are slightly different, there is perhaps one may say a remnant of a public intelligentsia — which we don't have here. We really do not have that here. We have some famous writers, who get published in all the journals, and then we have masses of people who are probably far more intelligent, far more creative, but who are not seen in the media and therefore are not seen to exist — sometimes even in their own eyes, and this is why I'm writing a book like *Immediatism:* to emphasize to the artist and the creative people that they do exist, they should exist in their own eyes, so what they do is important, even politically important; even though it happens outside the mass media in a sense is a blessing, not a curse. Things are slightly different in Europe perhaps for these reasons, but in America there's been very little crossover between my world and the world of media — and when I say that I don't even mean magazines and newspapers. I'm not even talking about television and advertising that are really mass media. I'm talking just about local newspapers. They're just not interested. There's no interest in political radicalism in intellectual circles in America, and I think it would be fair to say that — no interest whatsoever.

Q: In your text, you mentioned a certain psychic martial art and the return of the Paleolithic in the sense of a psychic technology which we forgot. Can you explain that?

A: Well, I'm really not trying to be so mysterious or to imply that there's a secret art which I know and which I'm not sharing. Why I called it a secret martial art is that it's simply secret because it's ignored or forgotten. What I mean to say is that living in the body, being aware of the positivity of the material bodily principle (to quote Bakhtin) is in fact a form of resistance, a martial art, if you will. In a world where the body is so degraded, so de-emphasized on the one hand by the empire of the image and on the other hand where the body is degraded by a kind of obsessive narcissism, athletics, fashion, and health, that somewhere in between these extremes to me is the ordinary body which, as the Zen masters would say, is the Zen body, to rephrase the saying that the ordinary mind is the Zen mind. To be conscious and aware of this is already to take a stance of resistance against the obliteration of the body in media or the pseudo-apotheosis of the body in modern sports, or fast food or all this kind of degradation of the body which occurs along with its erasure. So what would that art be I don't know exactly, I think it would be different for each person maybe, and certainly involve a kind of physical creativity that I discuss in the essays. Unfortunately, I haven't got it down to a science yet that could be taught in dojos and you get a black belt in it. It hasn't occurred yet, although perhaps some genius will come along and invent it.

Q: Do you get many invitations to parties that are strange for you or really come as a surprise because of who identifies with your stuff? Can you give examples?

A: I'll just give you one example. I was invited by a ceremonial magician who lives in a medieval castle in the south of France to come and see his museum of occult art. And this was simply as a result of his reading my work and corresponding with me for a while. It was great. I won't give his address, though.

Q: There's a lot of frank non-pessimism in what you write, and there's one chapter in your book about laughter as either a weapon or medicine. I was wondering who the people who would communicate this sort of healing laughter might be?

A: First of all, there's an existential choice involved here. I've always thought that literature should be entertaining as well as instructive — a very old-fashioned idea but one that I adhere to. When I set out to write in this way — particularly in this way, a political way, if you want to call it that — I intend to make a donation, to try to give something. There doesn't seem to me to be any point in giving more misery or exacerbating unhappiness through some kind of hyper-intellectual, pyrotechnical writing about unhappiness and the shit that we all find ourselves in. That's been done plenty. I think first of all that it doesn't need to be done any more and second of all there's a kind of reactionary aspect to it which is that the emphasizing of misery without any anti-pessimism, as you put it, would be simply seduction into inactivity and political despair. In other words, to do politics at all on any level, especially on a revolutionary or on an insurrectionary level, there has to be some anti-pessimism — I won't say optimism because that sounds so fatuous, futile; but anti-pessimism is a nice phrase. And there's a deliberate attempt at that in the writing. Then again it's a matter of my personality, I guess, inclined towards the notion of the healing laugh to some extent. We have an anarchist thinker in America, John Zerzan, who wrote an essay against humor which maybe is one of the things I was reacting against. Even if irony is counter-revolutionary which I think it might be to a certain extent I don't see any way in which you could say that laughter itself is counter-revolutionary. This doesn't make any sense to me unless you mean to get rid of language and thought altogether, which is just another form of nihilism. So as long as you're going to accept culture on some level you're certainly going to have to accept humor. And as long as you're going to have to accept humor you might as well see humor as potentially revolutionary. [...]

I'm actually not out to raise a lot of laughs. Humor can indeed become counter-revolutionary if it's simply exalted out of all proportion and made into the purpose or center of one's art. Well, this could perhaps be considered frivolity. Again, I would say that it's part of that natural martial art of the ordinary mind and body, it's just something that is, and therefore should be celebrated as part of existence.

Q: Palimpsest.

A: The whole idea behind palimpsest was to get over the fetish of the single original philosophy, the origin of single philosophies or the philosophy of single origins. I don't think that we should throw the idea of origins out the window, as for example is done in certain post-structuralist thinkers, or indeed really across the board in modern scientific discourse. In other words, origins are mythological, and comparative mythology still has a great deal to teach us, obviously. We still live in a world which generates mythology, even though people don't realize it. So origins are important, whether for positive or negative reasons, and my idea of the palimpsest was that it inscribes origins upon origins, and every origin that is potentially interesting should be added to the text, and although I don't literally write on top of writing — although it might be an interesting experiment — I do sort of encourage the readers to try to stack these origins or conceptual elements up in their minds as they read, and try to entertain them simultaneously. As the Red Queen told Alice in Wonderland, you have to entertain six impossible ideas before breakfast. This seems to me to be the best way to read. So there's that, but then on the other hand there's spontaneity, there's improvisation, there's the outflow of the moment, and so on, all of which are very important. But you know, I grew up in an era when improvisation really took over avantgarde art, especially theater and music and so forth, and I don't think the results were always very positive. When you improvise in a performance situation and you're not on, you're not brilliant, the results are totally disastrous, whereas at least if you had a plan, if you had some kind of structure that you're working with to begin with, you could at least turn it into a decent performance that would decently entertain everybody. So I tend to steer clear of improvisation as a principle, unless it's connected to really exalted consciousness in some department or another. Perhaps personally I tend more towards the palimpsest than to improvisation. I wouldn't necessarily want to separate them as a body-mind split.

Noise might even be a better concept than improvisation.

◆ MILLENNIUM ◆

(C. Loidl): Since I had the good fortune to meet you every now and then, I wonder what your mind is right now dwelling on. You always seem to be quite a bit ahead of your publications.

(H. Bey): I'm glad you asked. It's been over ten years since *TAZ* was witten and about five years since I worked on those essays on immediatism and I think quite a lot has changed. I'm just now working on an essay "Millennium" to try to update some of my thinking. Basically, I've recently come to feel that the collapse of the Communist world between 1989 and 1991 really marks the end of the century, so to speak. Of course, these are artificial divisions in history, but it still makes a kind of convenient way of thinking of it. And it's really taken me five years personally to figure out the implications of that for my own thinking. And the way I would express it now is that in TAZ and the Radio Sermonettes I was really proposing a third position, a position that was neither Capitalism nor Communism. This is basically, you could say, something that all Anarchist philosophy does. In this period I was telling it in my own way. It's a neither/nor position. It's a third position. Now, however, when you come to think about it, there are not two worlds any more or two possibilities or two contending opposing forces. There is in fact only one world, and that's the world of global capital. The world order, the world market, too-late capitalism, whatever you wanna call it, is now alone and triumphant. It's determinedly triumphant. It knows it's the winner although really it's only the winner by default, I think. And it tends to transform the world in its image. And that image, of course, is a monoculture based on Hollywood, on Disney, on commodities, on the destruction of the environment in every sense, from trees to imaginations, and the turning of all that into commodity, the turning of all that into money and the turning of money itself into a gnostic phantom-like experience which exists outside the world somewhere in a mysterious sphere of its own where money circulates, never descends, never reaches you and me. So what we're looking at is one single world. Obviously this one single world is not going to go without its revolution, it's not going to go without its opposition. And in fact it's around the word revolution that my thoughts are circulating now, because it seems to me that anarchists and anti-authoritarians in general can no longer occupy this third position; because how can you occupy a third position when there is no longer a second position? We can't talk about the Third World any more for the one reason that there's no second world. So even this third world as it used to be is now simply just the slums of the one world. It's just the no-go zone of that one single unified world of Capital. Obviously the communists are not going to step back into this position of opposition. Political Communism has completely shot its load, it's made itself look bad, taste bad in the mouth of history. No-one is calling on authoritarian Marxism to step back into this position of opposition. So where is this opposition supposed to come from? In my mind, first of all, this implies that if we're no longer trying to occupy a third position outside of this dichotomy, then WE are the opposition. Whether we know it or like it or not, we are the opposition. Now, who is we? For me the important thing is the realization that I have a new relation to the word revolution, whereas before I was inclined to look on it as a historical phantom, as in fact the lie told by Communism as opposed to the lie told by Capitalism. And whereas before I was extremely distrustful of the leftist dogma of revolution as opposed to the uprising or the insurrection, I would now say that history forces me once again to have to consider the idea of revolution and of myself as revolutionary and of my theory as revolutionary theory, because the opposition to the one world is already quite real. There is no way in which this triumph of capital can really & truly be a monolithic triumph excluding all difference from the world in the name of its sameness. And it looks to me like the revolutionary force in the single world of sameness has to be difference: revolutionary difference. And at the same time since the single world is involved, since the one world of capital is the world of separation, of alienation, that along with revolutionary difference it also has to be revolutionary presence (used to be called solidarity, although this is a word that presents some difficulties; I'd prefer simply the word "presence" as opposed to separation or absence.) So, I would say that the revolution of the present is a revolution for difference and for presence. It's opposed to sameness and separation. And as I look around the world to see where there might be arising a natural militant organisational form that speaks to this condition, the one shining example that I might be able to come up with would be the Zapatistas in Mexico, defending their right to be different, essentially. They want to be left alone in peace to be Mayan Indians, but they're not forcing anybody else to become Mayan Indians. They're not even suggesting it. They are different, but they're revolutionary. They are different, but they're in solidarity with all those people around the world who have come to support them, because their message is very new, it's very fresh and it attracts a lot of people: the idea that one can be different and revolutionary, that one can fight for social justice without the shadow of Moscow continually poisoning every action, etc.

This is something new in the world. *The New York Times* called it the first postmodern revolution, which was simply their sneering ironical way of trying to dismiss it, but in fact when you think about it, it is the first revolution of the 21st century in the terms that I began with, saying that we're already at the beginning of a new century, we're already if you like at the beginning of a millennium. And I expect to see many many more phenomena such as the Zapatistas. I would say that Bosnia potentially could have been such a phenomenon, not in the sense of an ethnic particularity like the Mayans, but in the sense of a pluralistic particularity: a small society where people were different but wanted to live together in peace. And this was seen to be perhaps even more dangerous than the Zapatista model, which is why in my view it was destroyed. It's possible that Bosnia may never be able to recreate itself again in the utopian way that it dreamed of in 1991. But that moment was there, and I think it has great significance for us. So, this to me is the line of the future. I think we have to reconsider all our priorities, we have to realize that militancy is once again a very important concept. This is not to say that I have any plan of march. I don't know what armies to join and am always suspicious of joining any army. But things have definitely changed. I'm embarrassed that it took me so long to figure it out. I don't think many people have really caught on to this yet. In fact, the fact that we still use words like "Third World" means that the popular language has not realized what happened in 1989–1991. So, the first goal is simply to try to raise consciousness about this and that's what I hope to do in the near future.

(D. Ender): Do you see any tangible effects of this lack of opposition in the USA?

(H. Bey): Oh yes, absolutely. The most tangible thing, and I think really the thing which gave me the clue to think about this, is precisely a psychic condition. One could point to lots of economic or social factors, but above all I feel a psychic malaise that is something quite new, and, well, a few years ago I began noticing in public speaking that there was a great deal less response on the part of audiences. You would get audiences that would sit there quite passively looking at you as if you were on television. And if questions came, they were very likely to be questions such as "Tell us what to do". You know when people ask you this sort of question they have no intention of actually taking your advice. What they're doing is trying to fill up some hole in themselves. So I thought, first of all it's just the influence of TV that's been around since 1947 or whatever, but then I realized that that's not a sufficient explanation for this kind of strange passivity. And I began hearing about it from other people who are involved in public speaking and then finally I read a whole section about it in Noam Chomsky's latest book. He has exactly the same experience of audiences, and all of these experiences begin around 1989, 1991. What I think has happened to us is not just TV. TV is just a symptom. So, what's happening is a kind of cognitive collapse around this single world. When people no longer feel a possibility in the world, a possibility of another position, then they become consciously opposed to the one. And conscious opposition is extremely difficult in an atmosphere that's completely poisoned by media such that no oppositional voice is ever really heard. Unless you yourself make the effort to get down to the alternative media, where that voice is still feebly speaking, then you're left simply in this one world of sameness and separation. Sameness — everything is the same; separation — every individual is separated from every other individual; complete alienation, complete unity. And I think that on the unconscious level, on the level of images, on the mythological level, on the religious level, if you wanna put it that way, this is what's happening, especially in America. I can't really speak of other places to the same degree. I've travelled in other countries, but one never has the sense of other countries the way one has the sense of one's own country. But I would imagine that it's a world-wide phenomenon — this kind of capitulation to the mono-culture on the deepest psychic level. So, yeah, it was in fact this sign which began to bother me to the point where I had to think my way through this problem of the one world, the two worlds, the three worlds and the revolutionary world. By no means have I finished thinking about it, but I recently had this — to me — this breakthrough about the word "revolution". So I see that as the only way to break through this particular wall of glass, this screen, yeah, to break through the screen.

C.L.: Sounds like a conclusion almost.

H.B.: Well, if you wish.

C.L.: No, not that I wish...When you talk about one or two or three or opposition and so on, I get totally contrary images to that in my head, because Europe right now and the further you go East in the Old World Europe, the more you see how it all has collapsed into little, almost tribal, very chauvinistic entities of people trying frantically to survive — the mafia is the very model — from that point of view and also from your talking about Too-Late Capitalism, I'd like to have an image of yours for how Europe as the EC or EU, which we're sitting right inside of right now, presents itself from over there.

H.B.: Well, obviously, especially from the breakdown of Communism you're going to get this smashing up into many little pieces. But it's more than that. We have to realize that difference is the organic revolutionary response to sameness and all of these splinter societies that you speak of consciously or unconsciously are revolutionary. Now, in the case of the Zapatistas or the Bosnians, let's say, this is a positive kind of revolution that we could support perhaps. In the case of the Serbians, it's something else. It's a conservative revolution, perhaps even a fascistic revolution. It's not really "nationalism", it's a form of ethnic imperialism. The point is that people are going to be emphasizing difference. Look at it this way: If you have your own culture, let's say it would be Bosnian Muslim or Finnish or Celtic or Ashanti or some tribal culture — this is going to become more and more precious to you as a source and a site of difference. This is where the difference is for you. It's in language, it's in cuisine, it's in art, it's in all of these things. The difference is that difference does not have to be hegemonistic or fascistic. And this is going to be extremely difficult for the old leftists to realize, because the old left itself had an ideal of a single world culture —

secular, rationalistic, you know, totally illumined, no shadows, industry, proletariat, forward into the future, basically extremely hegemonistic towards differences. Yes, they had their little Uzbeki folk-dancers, but this is simply a spectacle of difference, it's not true difference. And we have the same thing: we have 600 channels — choose one! There's a channel for everybody. Is this difference? No. This is not really difference. This is just sameness disguised as difference. But true organic integral difference is revolutionary, now. It has to be, because it's opposed to the single world, the mono-world, the mono-culture of capital. So, we have to choose and we have to influence other people's choices to go for an anti-hegemonistic particularity rather than a hegemonistic particularity. In other words, take the Zapatistas again as model here. As I said, they are not asking other people to become Mayan Indians. They are simply saying, "This is our difference. This is revolutionary for us. We are defending it." So it seems to me that what's happening in Europe on the one hand is this shattering into all of these fragments, which is a situation where political consciousness becomes extremely difficult. On the other hand, you have things like the EEU, which is simply, in my mind, symptomatic of capitalist mono-culture. So I guess that would mean, although I would have to think about this very carefully, I would say that a revolutionary stance in Europe would be anti-EEU. I think it would have to be, because the thing that we have to preserve is an ecology, you know. An ecology of mind and body implies difference. It implies differences in a state of balance — balance which can even include conflict. If you look at tribal societies, they are not necessarily peaceful societies. But the idea of war to the extinction of all individual desire — this is the monopoly of triumphant capital. And I think that it behooves us — we have to rethink our position if we consider ourselves as leftists of some sort or part of the leftist tradition in some way. We have to really seriously re-think our view of what revolutionary difference is, what it really could be. So, this to me is all inevitable. What's going on in Eastern Europe is inevitable and is potentially revolutionary. If it gets bogged down into conservative revolution and neo-fascism, this would be the great tragedy of the 21st century, but I don't think it's strictly speaking necessary. There is such a thing as revolutionary particularity. And as far as Eastern Europe goes, I would mention not only Bosnia as a failure, but maybe some other small enclaves as possible successes, you know. The anarchists in Ljubljana, they seem to be doing quite interesting things. It's a small enough country where they could have some real influence. So, interesting times ahead, no doubt about it.

C.L.: Yeah. Wish I could share your outlook on that.

H.B.: Go ahead and argue with me, because —

C.L.: No, no. What I saw much more was the latter part of what you said — the conservative capitalist revival in all those countries like Lithuania and Romania and so on. There was sort of a resistance spirit there, while there were those authoritarian governments. And now that those collapsed, it's like the Dollar is the main authority for everyone and it's everyone against everyone, and it's very hard to see anything revolutionary in that. Except that it looks like something very self-defeating.

H.B.: I agree with you, but Eastern Europe is the ideological battleground where capital wants to parade its triumph, where capital is determined to convert everybody. And of course, there's no doubt about it that sixty years of Communism made everybody extremely exhausted.

C.L.: And left them backwards also mentally. People have just been deprived of all sorts of information.

H.B.: I know exhaustion, but at the same time when I meet bright people from Eastern Europe, young intellectuals, punks, anarchists and so forth, I get the feeling of a kind of freshness of approach that's lacking in Western Europeans and Americans; because they were out of the loop for so long, because there is a certain perhaps even naiveté based on (laughter) ignorance. This can be turned into a kind of strength, too, in a paradoxical way. I mean, at conferences that I went to last year in Europe which mostly concerned the Internet and communication theory, always without exception the most interesting people were from Eastern Europe. They had the most to say, they had the most energy, the most creative ideas etc. etc. etc. So I don't think it's a totally grim and hopeless situation. I think that the power of international capital is very much focussed on that part of the world right now. So, resistance is extremely important. I think that it's a top priority for Americans and Western Europeans to show every kind of support for resistance in Eastern Europe. Whether it's going to work or not, who knows, you know. But what else have we got to do?

David Ender
Jack Hauser
Christian Loidl

♦ Millennium ♦

1. Jihad

When two set out to dine or duel together a third appears — *tertium quid*, parasite, witness, prophet, escapee. [See M. Serres, *Hermes.*]

Five years ago it still remained possible to occupy a third position in the world, a neither/nor of refusal or slyness, a realm outside the dialectic — even a space of withdrawal; — disappearance as will to power.

But now there is only one world — triumphant "end of History", end of the unbearable pain of imagination — actually an apotheosis of cybernetic Social Darwinism. Money decrees itself a law of Nature, and demands absolute liberty. Completely spiritualized, freed from its outworn body (mere production), circulating toward infinity & instantaneity in a gnostic numisphere far above Earth, money alone will define consciousness. The 20th century ended five years ago; this is the millennium. Where there is no second, no opposition, there can be no third, no neither/nor. So the choice remains: — either we accept ourselves as the "last humans", or else we accept ourselves as the opposition. (Either automonotony — or autonomy.) All positions of withdrawal must be re-considered from a point of view based on new strategic demands. In a sense, we're cornered. As the oldtime ideologues would have said, our situation is "objectively pre-revolutionary" again. Beyond the temporary autonomous zone, beyond the insurrection, there is the necessary revolution — the "jihad."

2. Sameness

21st century money is a chaos — while 20th century ideology was merely an entropy. Both bourgeois & anti-bourgeois thought proposed a single world — unified in consciousness by science — but money alone will actually achieve that world.

Money is not migratory, for the nomad moves from place to place while money moves from time to time, obliterating space. Money is not a rhizome but a chaos, an interdimensionality, inorganic but reproductive [infinite regressive bifurcation] — the sexuality of the dead.

"Capital," then, must be considered a "strange attractor." Perhaps the very mathematics of this money ("out of control") could already be traced in such esoteric webs as SWIFT, the private Internet for banks and arbitrage houses, where a trillion dollars a day disports itself in cyberspace (and less than 5% of it refers even obliquely to actual production).

The one world can deal with "chaos," but it reduces all true complexity to sameness & separation. Consciousness itself "enters into representation"; lived experience which demands presence must be denied lest it threaten to constitute another world beyond enclosure. In a heaven of imagery there persists only the afterlife of the screen, the gnostic stargate, the glass of disembodiment. Infinitely the same within an infinity of enclosures; infinitely connected yet infinitely alone. Immeasurable identity of desire, immeasurable distance of realization.

3. Management of Desires

The one world cannot package pleasure itself but only its image; malign hermeticism, a kind of *baraka* in reverse, the event horizon or terminal of desire. The "spirituality of pleasure" lies precisely in a presence that cannot be represented without disappearing; — inexpressible, unimpeachable, possible only in that "economy of the gift" that always exists (or is always re-invented) beneath the orthodoxy and paralysis of exchange. Desire is defined here as movement along such a trajectory — not as the itch that money can scratch.

Radical theory has recently developed a problematic of desire based on the perception that Capital is concerned with desire and able to satisfy it. Desire therefore is selfish and reactionary. But Benjamin has already shown that Capital's concern is precisely not to satisfy desire (i.e. to provide pleasure) but to exacerbate longing through the device of the "utopian trace" (the metaphysical shenanigans of the commodity, to paraphrase Marx). To say that capital liberates desire is a semantic absurdity based on a "mistranslation": — Capital liberates itself by enslaving desire. Fourier claimed that the twelve Passions — unrepressed — constitute the only possible basis for social Harmony. We may not follow his numerology, but we catch his drift.

Against the negative hermetism of the one world and its sham carnality, opposition proposes a gnosis of its own, a dialogics of presence, the pleasure of overcoming the representation of pleasure — a kind of touchstone. Not censorship, not management of the image, but the reverse — the liberation of the imagination from the empire of the image, from its overbearing omnipresence and singularity. The image alone is tasteless, like a bioindustrial tomato or pear — odorless as civilization itself, our "society of safety", our culture of mere survival. Ours is partly a struggle against colonial hearing & imperial gaze, and for smell, touch, taste — and for the "third eye".

If desire has disappeared into its representations then it must be rescued. Silence & secrecy are demanded, even a veiling of the image — ultimately a reenchantment of the forbidden. Only an eros that moves toward escape from enclosure within the banality of the image (and here, consciousness scarcely matters) can harmonize with the aesthetic of the jihad; whether it be expressed in conventional or unconventional roles or acts seems almost irrelevant.

Sexuality itself can be considered entheogenic — like the "sacred plants", it can provide not only cognitive structure but also imaginal content. The festal for us is at least a "serious joke" [an old definition of alchemy] if not a ritual necessity. "Enlightenment" is also a material bodily principle — and our secret is that our project need not be built exclusively on Nietzsche's "nothing".

4. Green Shade

Wild(er)ness stands for this very irreducibility of desire. The elimination of the non-human invokes the elimination of the human; culture can only be defined in relation to what it is not. Herein lies the profundity of paganism; in Islam, green is a heraldic color because "water, greenery, & a beautiful face" (as the Prophet said) are ontologically privileged in experience — and are in fact the basis of the esoteric rejection of sameness & separation — the divine as difference, immanent & immediate — not only in "Nature" but even in the garden or city as spontaneous organic crystallization of life's desire for itself. Perhaps all "real" wilderness has been disappeared into a cartomantic management of desires — after all, the one world knows no other — but if so, then its spectre haunts that world. It can be called back; it can be restored.

If Nature is de-natured in mediation's murderous museological gaze and if "everything" is mediated (even "direct sensory perception"), then how can we speak of restoration or of "immediacy"? First, because (in another manner of speaking) not everything has "entered into representation". The claim of the one world to its oneness is of course spurious — there persists by definition an outside to every enclosure in representation, not to mention a liminality around every border, an area of ambiguity. Oneness represents itself as invulnerable — but its weakness is revealed precisely in the moment of our perception that it is not reflected in lived experience; it shows itself in dislocation, hollowness, boredom, immiseration — this moment might constitute the "rending of the veil" that would allow a glimpse of the future, or at least of our desire for the future.

Second: we can speak here of restoration because not even every representation subsumed or produced within the enclosure of oneness can be considered effective in the service of repression. Language itself is haunted by the (sometimes unintentional) poetics of its own self-overcoming, by the subversive, the "eruption of the marvelous". Life seems to conspire with this outsideness, such that even representation finally escapes representation.

5. CASH

Green is made to symbolize the damned fertility of money, its contranatural fecundity — the alchemy of expropriation, the infinite weight of the privileged & Masonic gaze. In transcending its own textuality it becomes pure representation; from the very beginning however, from the first clay tokens or coins of electrum, money was already nothing but debt, nothing but absence.

Money "itself" retains a certain innocence as a simple medium of exchange — "poor" money, so to speak, stripped of interest in sheer circulation. At this level money might play its role even in the temporary autonomous zone; in relation to the jihad however money remains and must be considered under the sign of Capital as the measure of expropriation and the basic mytheme of separation.

And as money transcends its textuality in virtuality, interest can be extracted from each transaction, each disturbance of the aether; — "poor" money gives way to "pure" money. Who benefits?

The global machinery will never fall ripely into the hands of the insurgent masses, nor will its single Eye pass to the people (as if to one of three blind Fates); there will be no transition, smooth or bumpy, between Capitalism & some economic utopia, some miraculous salvation for the unified consciousness of post-Enlightenment rationalism & universal culture (with cozy corners for eccentric survivals & touristic bliss) — no Social Democracy taking over the controls in the name of the people. The "money-power" (as the old agrarians called it) is not in the power of an elite (whether conspiratorial or sociological) — rather the elite is in the power of money, like the hired human lackeys of some sci-fi AI entity in cyberspace.

Money-power is the global machinery — it can only be dismantled, not inherited. Will some sort of theoretical limit appear in the numisphere, so that the bubble bursts "on its own" as it were? Is Capitalism headed for the last round-up & final crisis to end all crises, or will it find a way to deal with & even profit by any "limits to growth" or chaotic perturbations within its closed atmosphere, its sphere of suffocation? [Stay Tuned.] In any case (to evoke Gustav Landauer) there is no "historical inevitability" about a revolution reborn in the very moment of Capital's triumphant closure of the dialectic.

[In one sense Capitalism seems to become "inevitable" in the invention of scarcity — the first moment of expropriation. But where precisely is this moment to be located? Agriculture is a great long-drawn-out crisis — but many horticultural-tribal societies remain as staunchly non-authoritarian & gift-oriented as the purest hunter/gatherers. Ancient hierarchic states (Sumer, Egypt, Shang China, etc.) and even feudalism still retain economies of reciprocity & redistribution; — the Market, as "predicted" by Classical Economics, simply fails to appear (see Karl Polyani). Moreover, every threat of its emergence is met with prescient resistance (as Clastres might have predicted): — separation & expropriation never go uncontested, and thus never appear in their absolute form. There exists in fact no natural law of circulation & exchange, no historical fatality, no destined atomicity of the social, and no unified world of representation. Capitalism exists — but not alone; revolution is its other. And vice versa.]

There is never a correct moment for declaring oneself in a state of rebellion. Perennial heretics, we have already made our choices — as if in some previous incarnation, or in some mythic time out of time, as if everything re-thinks itself in us or without us, and refusal were a kind of tepid pre-death, a resignation in morbidity. There is for us no return to innocence in the ecstasy of 600 channels, some dating back to the so-called "Fall of the Roman Empire" or even the early Neolithic. The very first emergences of separation in the earliest forms of money & the State created for us a tradition now some 10,000 years old — ultimately it doesn't matter whether "this is the crisis" or not. We would still choose.

6. Assault on the Screen

The media of sameness & separation represent the one world in its most religious form — the structuring of the social in images. Mere consciousness of this process cannot overcome it — opposition must also take a religious form in a reenchantment of counter-imagery; here one might speak of a rationalism of the marvellous. The only way to evade mere reaction (and thus subsumption into the image) would seem to lie in "sacralizing" our struggle against sameness & separation; — but only failure could induce us to accept the term "Romanticism" as critique (or praise) of our proposal.

Five years ago the media of sameness & separation attained much the same freedom & autonomy as the medium of money itself. Thus they shifted their emphasis from mere suppression to realization, and to the "interdisciplinary" boundary-breaking amalgamation of all modes of representation (from education to advertizing) into a single "polysemic" catastrophe of form: — the body slumped before the screen, all corporeality reduced to a darkness given shape only by light from the gnostic pleroma, that realm of transcendence from which bodies are exiled: — the heaven of glass.

The old Dualism has imploded into a totalized topology defined by the gnoseographic geosophy of money and its less-than-one dimensionality. The "mirror of production" has been superceded by a complete transparency, the vertigo of terror. Land, labor, nature, self itself, life itself, and even death can be re-invented as the basis of all exchange — everything is money.

[Note : Needless to say, these generalizations do

not concern the reality, but rather the ideology of global Capital (the ideology of the "post-ideological" con) — the intoxicated pronouncements of an "information economy" — the charade of "deregulation" (how can one speak of revolution when Capital has already broken all the rules?). Of course Capital has not really transcended production, but merely resituated it — somewhere near the realm of cemetery management or waste disposal. Capital wants ecstasy, not Taylorism; it longs for purity, for disembodiment.]

Ecstatic mediation finally blocks expression at the root, as for example in the biotechnological prosthesis or indifferentiation of body & screen. Mock nuptials of Eros & Thanatos: — terminal enclosure. The "greater jihad" of course is directed against the separated self — against suffocation of the true self that must express "its lord", its deepest meaning. But the "lesser jihad" is no less vital or imbued with baraka: — the assault on the screen.

7. THE MORALITY OF VIOLENCE

Any paradoxical reappearance of morality here will naturally begin on the ruins of orthodoxy — and pitch nothing more permanent there than the black tents of Ibn Khaldun's bedouin. And yet sooner or later *jihad* (struggle) leads back (via *ta'wil* or hermeneutic exegesis) to *shariah* or law. But shariah also means path or way — it is already the "open road" of the aimless wanderer. Values arise from imagination, i.e. from motion. "Where the gods have stopped" — this is the real. But the gods move on; they move, like light on water in Pindar's Odes.

The attentat is not immoral but simply impossible. The message of "terrorism" is that there's no there there; only the cybergnostic history-dump of sheer emptiness and anguish — limited liability as a cosmic principle. One might consider a morality (perhaps even an "imaginal morality") of violence against ideas & institutions — but the language lacks terms for such a form and thus dooms militancy to an indistinction of focus, even a deficit of attention. In any case it's not merely a question of one's "spiritual state" but of an actual auto-restructuring of cognition — not a state but a "station", in Sufi terms. To borrow a phrase from Ismailism, this is our version of the Da'wa al-Qadimi or the Ancient Propaganda — old because it is never quite fully born.

8. Fin de Siècle

There's nothing of futurity left to the concept of utopia. "Hope against hope"; no real choice is involved. Presence remains impure — only absence assumes the crystalline skeletal form of perfect eternity. A moral judgement if you like: intolerance for what opposes the jihad — but no more dandyism, no more brittle & elaborate constructions of the self.

Difference as identity constitutes a mode of expression as well as a mode of volition; there exists a tao of this process, a spontaneous ordering rather than an imperialist Cartesian gaze. This mode of expression as it pertains to culture (the "self-made" aspect of the social) either sets up an amplificatory resonance with "Nature" and is thus capable of changing the world-as-consensus — or else it is mere criminal stupidity.

Here again "mere" consciousness scarcely matters; hence there emerges for us an emphasis on non-ordinary states that overcome the dichotomy of self-reflective auto-intellection in concentrated attentiveness and in "skill". The self-closure of aesthetic or mental isolation denies the fact that every pleasure is an expansion, that reciprocity is non-predatory expansiveness. If revolt as expression responds to sameness & separation simultaneously, it constitutes by definition a movement toward difference & presence — and as the old phrenologists said, toward "communicativeness". That is, neither mere "communication" — subject to the drag of mediation & discorporealization — nor ecstatic "communion" (a term which smacks of the exacerbated authoritarianism of an enforced presence) — but rather a convivial connectivity — an eros of the social.

9. The Revolt of Islam

Proudhonian federalism based on non-hegemonic particularities in a "nomadological" or rhizomatic mutuality of synergistic solidarities — this is our revolutionary structure. (The very dryness of the terms itself suggests the need for an infusion of life into the theoryscape!) Post-Enlightenment ideology will experience queasiness at the notion of the revolutionary implications of a religion or way of life always already opposed to the monoculture of sameness & separation. Contemporary reaction will blanch at the idea of interpermeability, the porosity of solidarity, conviviality & presence as the complementarity & harmonious resonance of "revolutionary difference".

To take Islam as an example — the hyperorthodox & the ulemocracy cannot so easily reduce it to a hegemonistic/universalistic ideology as to rule out divergent forms of "sacred politics" informed by Sufism [e.g. the Naqshbandis], radical Shiism [e.g. Ali Shariati], Ismailism, Islamic humanism, the "Green Path" of Col. Qaddafi (part neo-Sufism, part anarcho-syndicalism), or even the cosmopolitan Islam of Bosnia. [Note: we mention these elements not to condone them necessarily, but to indicate that Islam is not a monolith of "fundamentalism".]

Traditions of tolerance, voluntaryism, egalitarianism, concern for social justice, critique of "usury", mystical utopianism — etc. — can form the constellations of a new propaganda within Islam, unshakably opposed to the cognitive colonialism of the numisphere, oriented to "empirical freedoms" rather than ideology, critical of repression within Islam, but committed to its creativity, reticence, interiority, militance, & style. Islam's concern with pollution of the imagination, which manifests in a literal veiling of the image, constitutes a powerful strategic realization for the jihad; — that which is veiled is not absent or invisible, since the veil is a sign of its presence, its imaginal reality, its power. That which is veiled is *unseen*.

10. VOLKWAYS

Tribal societies, left to their own devices, wage war in a manner not so much hegemonistic as adventuristic — and as P. Clastres pointed out, such horizontal warfare (like other "primitive" customs) actually militates against the emergence of "the

State" and its verticality: — violence as a form of resistance against separation, which is always felt by the tribe as a dangerous or "evil" possibility — violence as a form of the perennial fissipation or break-up & redistribution of power.

The jihad is not meant to be a return to this form of violence but a dialectical realization of its repressed content. This principle allows for a coalescence of variegated differences not just as a utopian construct but as a strategic bundling — as a "war machine".

Gustav Landauer makes clear that such groupings can themselves be considered both horizontally (or "federally") and vertically — not as categorical entifications, that is, but as volk, peoples, "nations" in the Native-american sense of the term. This concept was looted by base reaction and distorted into hegemonism of the worst sort, but it too can be rescued (an "adventure" in itself). [We need to re-read Proudhon, Marx, Nietzsche, Landauer, Fourier, Benjamin, Bakhtin, the IWW, etc. — the way the EZLN re-reads Zapata!]

Landauer also pointed out that the State is in part an inner relation, and not an absolute. Inasmuch as power shifts from the national map to "pure" Capital, the outer State becomes increasingly irrelevant as a focus of opposition. "Neutrality" is not an option: — either a zone is part of the one world, or it enters opposition. If the opposition zone coincides with certain political entities, then the revolution may have to consider political alliances. The greater jihad — against the inner relation of power — remains always the same; but the lesser jihad, against the outer relation, constantly changes shape.

[Note : Everything hinges on the perception that two forces — autonomy & federation — are not opposed but complementary or even complicit; if this is paradox, then it is paradox that must be lived. Ethnic cleansing & violent chauvinism are to be opposed from the point of view of federalism & solidarity because the hegemonism of such reaction simply reproduces the hegemonism (the cruelty) of the one world & even augments it. And authentic (non-hegemonic) difference must be defended because (or inasmuch as) it cannot or "should not" be obliterated by the Moloch of capitalist consciousness. Autonomy without federalism is at best implausible, at worst reactionary — but federalism without autonomy simply threatens the one value that unites the jihad — self-determination or "empirical freedom".]

For the strategic coalescence, complexity is not just an aesthetic but a necessity, a cognitive maquis or zone of resistance , a realm of ambiguity where the uprising must find its economy, its hearthlands. Every "nation" whether self-formed or traditional, and every group which moves horizontally within or across this milieu — councils, committees, unions, festivals — indeed, every "sovereign individual" — may consider federation on the basis of an ad-hoc anti-hegemonic front against the self-proclaimed totality of sameness & separation, and for a world of difference and presence.

From a certain viewpoint the force of presence or solidarity arises from the reality of "class" — although if we adopt that term we must consider the vast re-alignments and kaleidoscopic shifts of meaning that have unpacked & assembled it anew, stripped it of its 19th century accoutrements, its one-world telos & monocultural aesthetic — its scientism, its disenchantment, & its fatality. It's not just a question of the "proletarianization of the zones," but of the seamless and "natural" suppression of autonomous consciousness (and here, consciousness does matter).

11. Revolutionary Soteriology

Thus the "world to be saved" by the jihad consists not only of that Nature which cannot suffer final enclosure without the fatal estrangement of consciousness itself from all "original intimacy", but also the space of culture, of authentic becoming: — Tierra y Libertad. Agriculture may be considered as a tragic Fall from natural human economy — (gathering, hunting, reciprocity) — and even as a catastrophic shift in cognition itself. But to entertain the notion of its abolition involves a crypto-malthusian or even biophobic nihilism suspiciously akin to Gnostic suicide. The morality of substruction is already a morality of rescue (and vice versa); the kernel of the new society is always already forming within the shell of the old. Whatever the one world seeks to destroy or denigrate takes on for us the unmistakable aura of organic life; — this applies to the whole panoply of our present "late stone age", even its Fourierist refinements, even its surrealist urbanism (even "Civilization" might be considered a "good idea" if it could be released from its own predatory determinism); — this defines our conservativism. Thus despite everything, despite the titanic depredations of Capital's artificial intelligence, the "world to be saved" sometimes seems to differ from "this" world only by a hair's-breadth of satori. But it is entirely from this crack that our radical opposition emerges. The millennium is always the opening of a present moment — but it is also always the ending of a world.

12. The Hidden Imam

The jist of the jihad: when oppression takes the simultaneous & even paradoxical form of sameness & separation, then resistance or opposition logically proposes difference & presence — a revolutionary paradox. The rhizomatic segmentary society of identity that precipitates from this supersaturated logic of resistance can be contemplated from any angle, vertical or horizontal, diachronic or synchronic, ethnic or aesthetic — within the one necessary revolutionary anti-hegemonic principle of presence.

Our present state of flattened and irritable inattentiveness can only be compared to some esoteric medieval sin like spiritual sloth or existential forgetfulness; our first pleasure will be to imagine for ourselves a propaganda potent as the gnostic "Call", an aesthetic of repentance-&-conversion or "self-overcoming", a Sorelian mythos — a Millennium.

The blind panopticon of Capital remains, after all, most vulnerable in the realm of "magic" — the manipulation of images to control events, hermetic "action at a distance". If the tong provides a possible form for the new propaganda of the deed, then it must be confessed that mere aesthetic withdrawal (disappearance as will to power) cannot provide sufficient heat to hatch the egg of its secrecy. All that was once tertium quid is now (or will soon be) engaged either in capitulation or in opposition, as conflagration, as uprising against the management of desire & imagination within the englobed enclosure of the one world.

But in a pre-revolutionary situation the tactical advantage of clandestinity, of the unseen (the language of the heart), already restores to aesthetics its revolutionary centrality. The art of the unseen escapes absorption into the image-based "discourse of the totality" — and thus, alone of all possible forms, still holds out the millennial promise of art, the changing of the world.

[Note : The term "art" is being used here in two different senses: — the first sense is perhaps Romantic in that it addresses the dilemma of the artist per se & the problem of the "avant garde". But the second sense aims to dissolve the whole question of art's separateness in a practicum that is "normal" & that intersects (indeed almost coincides) with the realm of lived experience. The ordinary & the extraordinary are no longer opposed here, & are perhaps even in collusion, or in a dance of fused delineations. A crude truism: — the moment of the well-made is the very fabric of life itself, of life's saturation with itself; it is in this sense that traditional cultures could see no distinction between life & "art". If we were to speak of "political art", it could only be in the sense of an investigation of the fact that for us Capital defines itself in the context of a split between these things that "cannot" be separated. But this is a problem for every "worker", & not just for the "cultural worker" — & so in this sense, art begins to approach an area of identity with "revolutionary action".]

13. Call & Response

Less than a decade ago it was still possible to think of the "enemy" as the Planetary Work Machine, or the Spectacle — & therefore to think of resistance under the rubric of withdrawal or even escape. No great mysterious veil separated us from our will to imagine other forms of production, ludic & autonomous, or other forms of representation, authentic & pleasurable. The obvious goal was to form (or sustain) alternative nuclei based on the implementation of such forms, deploying resistance as a tactic in defense of these zones (whether temporary or permanent). In aikido there's no such thing as offense — one simply removes oneself from the force of an attack, whereupon the attacker's force turns against itself & defeats itself. Capitalism actually lost some ground to these tactics, in part because it was susceptible to "third force" strategies, and in part because as an ideology it remained unable to deal with its own inner contradictions ("democracy" for example).

Now the situation has changed. Capitalism is freed of its own ideological armoring & need no longer concede space to any "third force". Although the founder of aikido could dodge bullets, no one can stand aside from the onslaught of a power that occupies the whole extent of tactical space. Escapism is possible for the "third guest, the parasite" — but not for the sole opponent. Capitalism is now at liberty to declare war & deal directly as enemies with all former "alternatives" (including "democracy"). In this sense we have not chosen ourselves as opposition — we have been chosen.

In kendo it is said that there is no such thing as a defensive move, or rather that the only defense is a good offense. The attacker however has the disadvantage (imbalance) as in aikido: — so what to do? A paradox: when attacked, strike first. Clearly our "alternatives" are no longer merely interesting options, but life-or-death strategic positions. However, revolution is not a kendo match — nor a morality play. It would seem that our tactics will be defined not so much by history as by our determination to remain within history — not by "survival" but by persistence.

The "What Is To Be Done?" question must now be

begged for two reasons: — first, there already exist thousands of organizations working above-ground for de facto revolutionary goals (or at least for good causes) — but no organizing myth, no propaganda, no transformative "revolutionary consciousness" capable of transcending separation as reformist institutionalization & ideological sclerosis ["franchizing the issues"]. Second, most "illegalism" is frustratingly doomed to counterproductivity & recuperation for precisely the same reason — no consciousness, or rather, no metanoia, no unfragmented consciousness. In such a situation no coalescence seems feasible, and the jihad is faced first & foremost by the brutally theoretical need to comprehend & articulate its own historicity. To speak now of a "pre-revolutionary situation" smacks of the irony that such terms must inevitably invoke (history as "nightmare") — What signs have arisen, & on what horizon?

Here it should be recalled that "propaganda of the deed" was originally intended to include "good works" as well as violent ones; the temporary autonomous zone thus retains its value not only for its own sake but as a historicization of lived experience, perhaps even a mode of propaganda-in-action. The uprising could then be seen as the proposal of a "permanent autonomous zone"; and the coalescence of many such groups would make up the form of the "millennium". Here even "withdrawal" could have value as a tactic — provided it were coordinated & practised militantly on a mass scale — "revolutionary peace".

The very expression of such a scheme reveals at once how distant we remain from any realization. While we would like to indulge a crude existentialist penchant for "action", or at least for some sort of "anti-pessimism", any discussion of real tactics at this point might well prove fatally (or ludicrously) premature. Besides, "What should I do?" is perhaps the most mediated of questions, the one guaranteed to make any answer impossible.

* * * * * * * * * *

Such is our density that it's taken five years to figure this out. Everything that was once a "third path" must be re-thought in the light of one fact: — one world faces us, not two. If resistance has collapsed into bickering nostalgism (1968 has become as "tragic" for us as every other failure) — if leftist bitchiness & fascist particularism hold such an allure for exhausted radicals etc. — then it is because we have failed to articulate this one fact even to ourselves: — that by proclaiming itself absolute and by constructing a world on that proclamation, Capital has called back into being its old nemesis (so disgraced by the 20th century, so dead, so dull) — called it back into a whole new incarnation — as the last ditch defense of all that cannot be englobed — called back the revolution, the jihad.

> New York / Dublin
> Sept. 1, 1996

[Note : This version, not necessarily final, was arrived at with criticism & help from several groups: The Libertarian Book Club of New York, The Autonomedia editorial collective of Brooklyn, and The Garden of Delight in Dublin; the opinions however are my own, not theirs.]

◆ For and Against Interpretation ◆

> Angels are knocking at the tavern door
> — Hafez of Shiraz

> ...[to] the Lunaticks of Ireland...
> — Dean Swift's Last Will & Testament
> (formerly inscribed on the £10 note)

Kildare is flat — so no matter where you go you can see the electric lines parading across the landscape like Hollywood Martians. Patrick is staying at "Bishop's Court" which despite the name turns out to be a dank, three-room cottage and an old cowshed littered with artworks by Hilarius and others including several pieces made out of rusty farm implements and slabs of peat cut from local bog. After tea in the windswept muddy farmyard, we set out to find St. Patrick's Church and Well, not far away in another farmyard next to a metal barn and surrounded by cows and cowshit — thirteenth century or earlier, Romanesque with a touch of Gothic (or Egyptian?) in the pointed arch of the windows — restored in the 1950s but forgotten and overgrown with ivy and cobwebs — the architecture enforces humility since one must stoop to enter as in Zen tea-houses. Our friends James and Sean have decided to spruce it up, construct an altar and hang a brass bell in the belfry, then see how long it takes for anyone to notice. We walk along the road occasionally cringing into the wildflowers, to dodge the fast cars of big farmers, then duck into the hedge of blackberry vines full of late flowers and early fruit. The Well doesn't appear to be listed in any national Register — perhaps no one visits it anymore. Like other springs I've seen in Ireland, it feels like a sapphire set in an emerald set in jade, set in a druid's hand — we circle it thrice sunwise then drink — cars are whizzing by not twenty paces away — Sean recently saw a spirit here and left a portrait of it like a life-mask in plaster next to the Well on a slab of stone.

According to the 13th century Andalusian Sufi Ibn Arabi there exist "delicate tenuities" that stretch between heaven and earth like Jacobs-ladders — and the "meanings" which descend along these tenuities are like angels. I believe he actually saw the tenuities as nearly-transparent ribbands of light, strands of aurora borealis pulsing with luminous nodes like stars falling through gauze curtains. There's no need to limit this perception either by theological or psychological explanations — for the naive realist any experience has as much a priori claim to ontological authenticity as any other experience — a spirit is seen or a meaning descends in the same manner that a soft rain is seen and descends. But how naive can we be? Never mind — the most advanced science or abstruse theology leads us in bewilderment back to the same crude existentialist proposal: since it appears, it might as well be real. So — if the meaning that appears in the tenuity is real, it can be traced back to its source which is real — or real enough for our present purposes — and this tracing-back is called (by the Ismaili gnostics) *ta'wil,* or "Interpretation." The psychologist would say the knowledge that arises in this operation comes from inside — the theologian would say it comes from outside — but for us both explanations have lost power to beguile. As an alchemical process, interpretation transpires in a space both inside/outside and neither simultaneously; as "hermeneutic exegesis" (in Henry Corbin's phrase) it belongs to an in-between or isthmus called Mundus Imaginalis, where images appear as autonomous, or where dreams foretell the truth. In one sense neither real nor unreal, in another sense, perfectly capable of appearing to us as spirit, the world of the imagination acts as if it were the source of significances, location of personae, breath of the world. Science and religion might unite to call this delusion — but for us it is rather a matter of sheer desperation. The two-dimensionality of duelling epistemologies, dichotomies, semantic traps, bad faiths — fuck science and religion — we should demand a rationalism of the marvellous — an end to the violence of the explanation.

In this context, individuals and groups bear the responsibility of making contact with their own angels — even the mystic gurus have misled us here, since they stand between us and our own awareness and pretend to an authority that reduces us to subjects — or rather to objects — objects of someone else's interpretation. It seems we cannot escape the imputation of an old heresy here — based on the presumption that everyone at every moment knows precisely what's going on and what to do — if only they can break free of need, oppression, and the suffocation of false consciousness — and escape the scarcity by which authority measures its wealth and its power against us. Above all — the scarcity of interpretation.

The most pernicious power of interpretation belongs now to Capital itself, which claims to be free of all dualities, all otherness — in a terminal "obscene ecstasy" of unified and flattened consciousness — a universalization of money in conceptual space, far removed and transcendent above all mere filthy production, a kind of numisphere or heavenly weather of pure money — and in global debt, everything's debt to nothing, like a black hole on the event horizon, sucking up every last particle of light into an emptiness beyond history. According to the "natural law" of this total liberation of money, nothing — not even air, water, or dirt — is to be experienced directly by the autonomous self or group; everything must be mediated by money itself, which intends to stand between consciousness and production as an absolute filter, sifting out every last trace of authenticity and charging for it — taxing reality itself — as an ultimate power beyond even authority or law. Above all, Capital intends to acquire a monopoly of interpretation.

Walter Benjamin has elucidated the process whereby the commodity is imbued with a "utopian trace" — that is, by the image of a promise: that this object-for-sale contains a kind of futurity or no-place-place where your consciousness will once more be valid, your experience real. If the product were not so advertized, you would not buy it — but if the product delivered its promise, you would stop buying other products — why go on spending money once realization is attained? — and thus cause the collapse of Capitalism. Money can only circulate freely in a realm of continual disappointment — the reproduction of scarcity is the production of wealth. I am only rich if others are poor — but money itself has no other end or goal than the total poverty of everything that is not "the Market." Having long ago capitalized all material being, the power of scarcity has had no choice but to commodify the image (and the imagination) as well — on the presumption that this is an ever-expanding market. Awareness must be privatized — thought must be appropriated, adulterated, alienated, packaged, labelled, advertized and sold back to consciousness. All creativity must be priced, and even the very process of resistance against this expropriation must be turned to profit ("Be a rebel — buy a Toyota!" — or "Image is nothing, taste is everything" as a slogan for some crappy softdrink). All informational media from education to advertizing are dedicated to detaching the image from any mooring in experienced life, floating it free, and re-materializing it in commodification. Work, consume, die.

Tourism is perfect Capitalism: the consumption of the image of the world as it really is — the chief goods on sale include geography (the inscription of significance in the landscape) and historiography (the inscription of meaning in the culturescape). But the ultimate image is that of the "blessing" or baraka inherent in the object of the tourist's gaze. The possible moment of realization is packaged, pre-interpreted by official experts, transformed into a series of views, distanced from the direct senses (touch, taste, smell); space is overwhelmed by time, stratified, separated, parcelled on a grid of permissible expectations; becoming is rendered into the rigid digitalizations of recording devices, banished from memory, and embalmed into a counterfeit of pure being. So-called primitives would say that soul is being stolen here, that meaning itself has entered a field of decay, a sort of beam emanating from an evil eye or withered self eaten by envy of all significance. The problem lies not in the content of the tourist's experience — one can imagine tours based on ideas we might consider quite correct or even beautiful — the problem is inherent in the container, in the very fact of interpretation, in the structure of a "dialogue" that excludes all response, resonance, or resistance. Certain kinds of travel — nomadism, pilgrimage — return meaning to the landscape. Other kinds — war, tourism — can only take it away. Reciprocity reaches a vanishing point in such patterns of depredation. Even the most subtle propaganda of the State never approached this ultimate edge — after all, it always evoked its own opposition — while tourism represents the end of all dialectic — since the only negative gesture it evokes is terrorism, which is its own suppressed content, its "evil twin". The tourist, seduced by the utopian trace in its most poignant aspect — the image of difference — becomes a molecule of pollution, bears the virus of sameness, and the burden of disappointment, into a world that once lived for itself.

The role of the artist in Capitalism can be compared with that of the tour-guide: — interpreter of experience for consumption on the most elite level, agent of recuperation for society's most exquisite longings or deepest resentments; — and even a tour-guide may be sincere. But the comparison might prove invidious — inasmuch as the artist's intention is to add meaning to the sum total of experience, not to subtract or abstract it. The gesture art makes presupposes the gesture of reciprocity, of presence. This movement is interrupted by the essentially non-human intervention of Capital, the exacerbated mediation of a power that can only grow by creating scarcity and separation. What if all the artists, poets, scholars and musicians of Ireland were invited to transform the country's new Interpretive Centres in their own image? Who cares what exalted aesthetic lays claim to the triumph of interpretation so long as the result is always the suppression of our own creativity? In Java, I heard that "Everyone must be an artist" — and indeed everyone already is an artist to the extent that all lived experience is a co-creation of self and other: — production that is also play — and above all, the production of meaning. We do not need the artist to live for us, but simply to be our facilitator, our companion, part of our circle of reciprocity — and as for art, if there exists any way for it to avoid being englobed, we can see it only as a form of opposition to the One Big World of unified representation. Such art refuses to become part of the Grand Unified Theory of the end of physics or history or the minimum wage or anything else. There's nothing "virtual" about it — and it's not headed for a condition of "disappearance," which would simply amount to defeat. I believe modern art as resistance is headed for the condition of the Unseen. That which is real but not seen has the power of the occult, of the imagination, of the erotic — like Sean's spirit-mask at Patrick's Well, it gives back meaning to the landscape — it abides unnoticed until someone perhaps takes it as a free gift — by its very existence it challenges the world of the commodified image and changes (however slightly) the shape of consensus reality. Even at its most hidden and secret, it exercises a magnetic effect, brings about subtle shifts and re-alignments — and at least in theory, it gives up merely talking about the world in order to change it. Is this perhaps however covertly an authoritarian act? No, not if it were a sharing of meaning, an opening into the field of "delicate tenuities". What if it were rendered completely invisible? Then perhaps we might speak of the presence of spirits, of a necessary re-enchantment too tenuous for the imperial heaviness of the eye — and of a necessary clandestinity. And what if it were to re-appear sometime as sheer opposition to the unbreathing virtuality of a world which is always deferred, always someplace else, always fatal?

That evening we drive back to Dublin in the long summer light past megalithic mounds, travellers' encampments, and the crumbling 18th century follies and ziggurats of mad Ascendency lords — past St. Patrick's Hospital, which Dean Swift left in his will "to the lunaticks of Ireland" — sites that have perhaps not yet been absorbed into the new world of Euro-money, golf, and the National Heritage. Just before nightfall, we're in Dun Laoghaire near the Martello tower, looking out at a heavy and nostalgic view of the ocean under gray clouds. The front gardens of the seedy Victorian seaside villas are adorned with one of my favorite Irish plants, mysterious and rather shabby palmtrees that evoke for me a secret Moorish past, a memory of Barbary corsairs, or of monks from Egypt and Spain. A Celtic cross was once discovered in Ireland engraved with the Arabic phrase "Bismillah," the opening of the Koran. These palmtrees were probably introduced by some turn-of-the-century horticulturalist with a taste for the exotic, but for me they stand for Ireland's "hidden African soul." A soft dark rain begins to fall. Or that at least is my interpretation.

Dublin, Aug. 23, 1996

◆ Religion and Revolution ◆

Real money & hierarchic religion appear to have arisen in the same mysterious moment sometime between the early Neolithic and the third millennium BC in Sumer or Egypt; which came first, the chicken or the egg? Was one a response to the other or is one an aspect of the other?

No doubt that money possesses a deeply religious implication since from the very moment of its appearance it begins to strive for the condition of the spirit — to remove itself from the world of bodies, to transcend materiality, to become the one true efficacious symbol. With the invention of writing around 3100 BC money as we know it emerges from a complicated system of clay tokens or counters representing material goods & takes the form of written bills of credit impressed on clay tablets; almost without exception these "cheques" seem to concern debts owed to the State Temple, & in theory could have been used in an extended system of exchange as credit-notes "minted" by the theocracy. Coins did not appear until around 700 BC in Greek Asia Minor; they were made of electrum (gold and silver) not because these metals had commodity value but because they were sacred — Sun & Moon; the ratio of value between them has always hovered around 14:1 not because the earth contains 14 times as much silver as gold but because the Moon takes 14 "suns" to grow from dark to full. Coins may have originated as temple tokens symbolizing a worshipper's due share of the sacrifice — holy souvenirs, which could later be traded for goods because they had "mana", not use-value. (This function may have originated in the Stone Age trade in "ceremonial" stone axe-heads used in potlach-like distribution rites.) Unlike Mesopotamian credit-notes, coins were inscribed with sacred images & were seen as liminal objects, nodal points between quotidian reality & the world of the spirits (this accounts for the custom of bending coins to "spiritualize" them and throwing them into wells, which are the "eyes" of the otherworld.) Debt itself — the true content of all money — is a highly "spiritual" concept. As tribute (primitive debt) it exemplifies capitulation to a "legitimate power" of expropriation masked in religious ideology — but as "real debt" it attains the uniquely spiritual ability to reproduce itself as if it were an organic being. Even now it remains the only "dead" substance in all the world to possess this power — "money begets money". At this point money begins to take on a parodic aspect vis-a-vis religion — it seems that money wants to rival god, to become immanent spirit in the form of pure metaphysicality which nevertheless "rules the world". Religion must take note of this blasphemous nature in money and condemn it as contra naturam. Money & religion enter opposition — one cannot serve God & Mammon simultaneously. But so long as religion continues to perform as the ideology of separation (the hierarchic State, expropriation, etc.) it can never really come to grips with the money-problem. Over & over again reformers arise within religion to chase the moneylenders from the temple, & always they return — in fact often enough the moneylenders become the Temple. (It's certainly no accident that banks for a long time aped the forms of religious architecture.) According to Weber it was Calvin who finally resolved the issue with his theological justification for "usury" — but this scarcely does credit to the real Protestants, like the Ranters & Diggers, who proposed that religion should once & for all enter into total opposition to money — thereby launching the Millennium. It seems more likely that the Enlightenment should take credit for resolving the problem — by jettisoning religion as the ideology of the ruling class & replacing it with rationalism (& "Classical Economics"). This formula however would fail to do justice to those real illuminati who proposed the dismantling of all ideologies of power & authority — nor would it help to explain why "official" religion failed to realize its potential as opposition at this point, & instead went on providing moral support for both State & Capital.

Under the influence of Romanticism however there arose — both inside & outside of "official" religion — a growing sense of spirituality as an alternative to the oppressive aspects of Liberalism & its intellectual/artistic allies. On the one hand this sense led to a conservative-revolutionary form of romantic reaction (e.g. Novalis) — but on the other hand it also fed into the old heretical tradition (which also began with the "Rise of Civilization" as a movement of resistance to the theocracy of expropriation) — and found itself in a strange new alliance with rationalist radicalism (the nascent "left"); William Blake, for example, or the "Blaspheming Chapels" of Spence & his followers, represent this trend. The meeting of spirituality & resistance is not some surrealist event or anomaly to be smoothed out or rationalized by "History" — it occupies a position at the very root of radicalism; — and despite the militant atheism of Marx or Bakunin (itself a kind of mutated mysticism or "heresy"), the spiritual still remains inextricably involved with the "Good Old Cause" it helped create.

Some years ago Regis Debray wrote an article pointing out that despite the confidant predictions of 19th century materialism, religion had still perversely failed to go away — and that perhaps it was time for the Revolution to come to terms with this mysterious persistence. Coming from a Catholic culture Debray was interested in "Liberation Theology", itself a projection of the old quasi-heresy of the "Poor" Franciscans & the recurrent rediscovery of "Bible communism". Had he considered Protestant culture he might have remembered the 17th century, & looked for its true inheritance; if Moslem he could have evoked the radicalism of the Shiites or Ismailis, or the anti-colonialism of the 19th century "neo-Sufis". Every religion has called forth its own inner antithesis over & over again; every religion has considered the implications of moral opposition to power; every tradition contains a vocabulary of resistance as well as capitulation to oppression. Speaking broadly one might say that up until now this "counter-tradition" — which is both inside & outside religion — has comprised a "suppressed content". Debray's question concerned its potential for realization. Liberation Theology lost most of its support within the church when it could no longer serve its function as rival (or accomplice) of Soviet Communism; & it could no longer serve this function because Communism collapsed. But some Liberation theologians proved to be sincere — and still they persist (as in Mexico); moreover, an entire submerged & related tendency within Catholicism, exemplified in the almost Scholastic anarchism of an Ivan Illich, lingers in the background. Similar tendencies could be identified within Orthodoxy (e.g. Bakhtin), Protestantism, Judaism, Islam, and (in a somewhat different sense) Buddhism; moreover, most "surviving" indigenous forms of spirituality (e.g. Shamanism) or the Afroamerican syncretisms can find common cause with various radical trends in the "major" religions on such issues as the environment, & the morality of anti-Capitalism. Despite elements of romantic reaction, various New Age & post-New-Age movements can also be associated with this rough category.

In a previous essay we have outlined reasons for believing that the collapse of Communism implies the triumph of its single opponent, Capitalism; that according to neo-liberal global propaganda only one world now exists; & that this political situation has grave implications for a theory of money as the virtual deity (autonomous, spiritualized, & all-powerful) of the single universe of meaning. Under these conditions everything that was once a third possibility (neutrality, withdrawal, counter-culture, the "Third

World", etc.) now must find itself in a new situation. There is no longer any "second" — how can there be a "third"? The "alternatives" have narrowed catastrophically. The One World is now in a position to crush everything which once escaped its ecstatic embrace — thanks to the unfortunate distraction of waging an essentially economic war against the Evil Empire. There is no more third way, no more neither/nor. Everything that is different will now be subsumed into the sameness of the One World — or else will discover itself in opposition to that world. Taking this thesis as given, we must now ask where religion will locate itself on this new map of "zones" of capitulation & resistance. If "revolution" has been freed of the incubus of Soviet oppression and is now once again a valid concept, are we finally in a position to offer a tentative answer to Debray's question?

Taking "religion" as a whole, including even those forms such as shamanism that belong to Society rather than the State (in terms of Clastres's anthropology); including polytheisms, monotheisms, & non-theisms; including mysticisms & heresies as well as orthodoxies, "reformed" churches, & "new religions" — obviously the subject under consideration lacks definition, borders, coherence; & it cannot be questioned because it would only generate a babel of responses rather than an answer. But "religion" does refer to something —

call it a certain range of colors in the spectrum of human becoming — & as such it might be considered (at least pro tem) as a valid dialogic entity & as a theorizable subject. In the triumphant movement of Capital — in its processual moment so to speak — all religion can only be viewed as nullity, i.e. as a commodity to be packaged & sold, an asset to be stripped, or an opposition to be eliminated. Any idea (or ideology) that cannot be subsumed into capital's "End of History" must be doomed. This includes both reaction & resistance — & it most certainly includes the non-separative "re-linking" (religio) of consciousness with "spirit" as unmediated imaginal self-determination & value-creation — the original goal of all ritual & worship. Religion in other words has lost all connection with worldly power because that power has migrated off-world — it has abandoned even the State & achieved the purity of apotheosis, like the God that "abandoned Anthony" in Cavafy's poem. The few States (mostly Islamic) wherein religion holds power are located precisely within the ever-shrinking region of national opposition to Capital — (thus providing them with such potential strange bedfellows as Cuba!). Like all other "third possibilities" religion is faced with a new dichotomy: total capitulation, or else revolt. Thus the "revolutionary potential" of religion clearly appears — although it remains unclear whether resistance might take the form of reaction or radicalism — or indeed whether religion is not already defeated — whether its refusal to go away is that of an enemy, or a ghost.

In Russia & Serbia the Orthodox Church appears to have thrown in its lot with reaction against the New World Order & thus found new fellowship with its old Bolshevik oppressors. In Chechnya the Naqshbandi Sufi Order continues its centuries-old struggle against Russian imperialism. In Chiapas there's a strange alliance of Mayan "pagans" & radical Catholics. Certain factions of American Protestantism have been driven to the point of paranoia & armed resistance (but even paranoids have some real enemies); while Native-american spirituality undergoes a small but miraculous revival — not a Ghost Shirt uprising this time, but a reasoned & profound stand against the hegemony of Capital's monoculture. The Dalai Lama sometimes appears as the one "world leader" capable of speaking truth both to the remnants of Communist oppression & the forces of Capitalist inhumanity; a "Free Tibet" might provide some kind of focus for an "interfaith" bloc of small nations & religious groups allied against the transcendental social darwinism of the consensus. Arctic shamanism may re-emerge as an "ideology" for the self-determination of certain new Siberian republics — and some New Religions (such as Western neo-paganism or the psychedelic cults) also belong by definition or default to the pole of opposition.

Islam has seen itself as the enemy of imperial Christianity & European imperialism almost from the moment of its inception. During the 20th century it functioned as a "third way" against both Communism & Capitalism, & in the context of the new One World it now constitutes by definition one of the very few existing mass movements which cannot be englobed into the unity of any would-be Consensus. Unfortunately the spearhead of resistance — "fundamentalism" — tends to reduce the complexity of Islam into an artificially coherent ideology — "Islamism" — which clearly fails to speak to the normal human desire for difference & complexity. Fundamentalism has already failed to concern itself with "empirical freedoms" which must constitute the minimal demands of the new resistance; for example, its critique of "usury" is obviously an inadequate response to the machinations of the IMF & World Bank. The "gates of Interpretation" of the Shariah must be re-opened — not slammed shut forever — and a fully-realized alternative to Capitalism must emerge from within the tradition. Whatever one may think of the Libyan Revolution of 1969 it has at least the virtue of an attempt to fuse the anarcho-syndicalism of '68 with the neo-Sufi egalitarianism of the North African Orders, & to create a revolutionary Islam — something similar could be said of Ali Shariati's "Shiite socialism" in Iran, which was crushed by the ulemocracy before it could crystallize into a coherent movement. The point is that Islam cannot be dismissed as the puritan monolith portrayed in the Capitalist media. If a genuine anti-Capitalist coalition is to appear in the world it cannot happen without Islam. The goal of all theory capable of any sympathy with Islam, I believe, is now to encourage its radical & egalitarian traditions & to substruct its reactionary & authoritarian modes of discourse. Within Islam there persist such mythic figures as the "Green Prophet" and hidden guide of the mystics, al-Khezr, who could easily become a kind of patron saint of Islamic environmentalism; while history offers such models as the great Algerian Sufi freedom-fighter Emir Abdul Qadir, whose last act (in exile in Damascus) was to protect Syrian Christians against the bigotry of the ulema. From outside Islam there exists the potential for "interfaith" movements concerned with ideals of peace, toleration, & resistance to the violence of post-secular post-rationalist "neo-liberalism" & its allies. In effect, then, the "revolutionary potential" of Islam is not yet realized — but it is real.

Since Christianity is the religion that "gave birth" (in Weberian terms) to Capitalism, its position in relation to the present apotheosis of Capitalism is necessarily more problematic than Islam's. For centuries Christianity has been drawing in on itself & constructing a kind of make-believe world of its own, wherein some semblance of the social might persist (if only on Sundays) — even while it maintained the cozy illusion of some relation to power. As an ally of Capital (with its seeming benign indifference to the hypothesis of faith) against "Godless Communism", Christianity could preserve the illusion of power — at least until five years ago. Now Capitalism no longer needs Christianity & the social support it enjoyed will soon evaporate. Already the Queen of England has had to consider stepping down as the head of the Anglican Church — & she is unlikely to be replaced by the CEO of some vast international zaibatsu! Money is god — God is really dead at last; Capitalism has realized a hideous parody of the Enlightenment ideal. But Jesus is a dying-&-resurrecting god — one might say he's been through all this before. Even Nietzsche signed his last "insane" letter as "Dionysus & the Crucified One"; in the end it is perhaps only religion that can "overcome" religion. Within Christianity a myriad tendencies appear (or have persisted since the 17th century, like the Quakers) seeking to revive that radical messiah who cleansed the Temple & promised the Kingdom to the poor. In America for instance it would seem impossible to imagine a really successful mass movement against Capitalism (some form of "progressive populism") without the participation of the churches. Again the theoretical task begins to clarify itself; one need not propose some vulgar kind of "entryism" into organized Christianity to radicalize it by conspiracy from within. Rather the goal would be to encourage the sincere & widespread potential for Christian radicalism either from within as an honest believer (however "existentialist" the faith!) or as an honest sympathizer from the outside.

To test this theorizing take an example — say Ireland (where I happen to be writing this). Given that Ireland's "Problems" arise largely from sectarianism, clearly one must take an anti-clerical stance; in fact atheism would be at least emotionally appropriate. But the inherent ambiguity of religion in Irish history should be remembered: — there were moments when Catholic priests & laity supported resistance or revolution, & there were moments when Protestant ministers & laity supported resistance or revolution. The hierarchies of the churches have generally proven themselves reactionary — but hierarchy is not the same thing as religion. On the Protestant side we have Wolfe Tone & the United Irishmen — a revolutionary "interfaith" movement. Even today in Northern Ireland such possibilities are not dead; anti-sectarianism is not just a socialist ideal but also a Christian ideal. On the Catholic side...a few years ago I met a radical priest at a pagan festival in the Aran Islands, a friend of Ivan Illich. When I asked him, "What exactly is your relation to Rome?" he answered, "Rome? Rome is the enemy." Rome has lost its stranglehold on Ireland in the last few years, brought down by anti-puritan revolt & internal scandal. It would be incorrect to say that the Church's power has shifted to the State, unless we also add that the government's power has shifted to Europe, & Europe's power has shifted to international capital. The meaning of Catholicism in Ireland is up for grabs. Over the next few years we might expect to see both inside & outside the Church a kind of revival of "Celtic Christianity" — devoted to resistance against pollution of the environment both physical & imaginal, & therefore committed to anti-Capitalist struggle. Whether this trend would lead to an open break with Rome and the formation of an independent church — who knows? Certainly the trend will include or at least influence Protestantism as well. Such a broad-based movement might easily find its natural political expression in socialism or even in anarcho-socialism, & would serve a particularly useful function as a force against sectarianism & the rule of the clerisy. Thus even in Ireland it would seem that religion may have a revolutionary future.

I expect these ideas will meet with very little acceptance within traditionally atheist anarchism or the remnants of "dialectical materialism".

Enlightenment radicalism has long refused to recognize any but remote historical roots within religious radicalism. As a result, the Revolution threw out the baby ("non-ordinary consciousness") along with the bathwater of the Inquisition or of puritan repression. Despite Sorel's insistence that the Revolution needed a "myth", it preferred to bank everything on "pure reason" instead. But spiritual anarchism & communism (like religion itself) have failed to go away. Indeed, by becoming an anti-Religion, radicalism had recourse to a kind of mysticism of its own, complete with ritual, symbolism, & morality. Bakunin's remark about God — that if he existed we would have to kill him — would after all pass for the purest orthodoxy within Zen Buddhism! The psychedelic movement, which offered a kind of "scientific" (or at least experiential) verification of non-ordinary consciousness, led to a degree of rapprochement between spirituality & radical politics — & the trajectory of this movement may have only begun. If religion has "always" acted to enslave the mind or to reproduce the ideology of the ruling class, it has also "always" involved some form of entheogenesis ("birth of the god within") or liberation of consciousness; some form of utopian proposal or promise of "heaven on earth"; and some form of militant & positive action for "social justice" as God's plan for the creation. Shamanism is a form of "religion" that (as Clastres showed) actually institutionalizes spirituality against the emergence of hierarchy & separation — & all religions possess at least a shamanic trace.

Every religion can point to a radical tradition of some sort. Taoism once produced the Yellow Turbans — or for that matter the Tongs that collaborated with anarchism in the 1911 revolution. Judaism produced the "anarcho-zionism" of Martin Buber & Gersholm Scholem (deeply influenced by Gustav Landauer & other anarchists of 1919), which found its most eloquent & paradoxical voice in Walter Benjamin. Hinduism gave birth to the ultra-radical Bengali Terrorist Party — & also to M. Gandhi, the modern world's only successful theorist of non-violent revolution. Obviously anarchism & communism will never come to terms with religion on questions of authority & property; & perhaps one might say that "after the Revolution" such questions will remain to be resolved. But it seems clear that without religion there will be no radical revolution; the Old Left & the (old) New Left can scarcely fight it alone. The alternative to an alliance now is to watch while Reaction coöpts the force of religion & launches a revolution without us. Like it or not, some sort of pre-emptive strategy is required. Resistance demands a vocabulary in which our common cause can be discussed; hence these sketchy proposals.

Even assuming we could classify all the above under the rubric of admirable sentiments, we would still find ourselves far from any obvious program of action. Religion is not going to "save" us in this sense (perhaps the reverse is true!) — in any case religion is faced with the same perplexity as any other former "third position", including all forms of radical non-authoritarianism & anti-Capitalism. The new totality & its media appear so pervasive as to fore-doom all programs of revolutionary content, since every "message" is equally subject to subsumption in the "medium" that is Capital itself. Of course the situation is hopeless — but only stupidity would take this as reason for despair, or for the terminal boredom of defeat. Hope against hope — Bloch's revolutionary hope — belongs to a "utopia" that is never wholly absent even when it is least present; & it belongs as well to a religious sphere in which hopelessness is the final sin against the holy spirit: — the betrayal of the divine within — the failure to become human. "Karmic duty" in the sense of the Bhagavad Gita — or in the sense of "revolutionary duty" — is not something imposed by Nature, like gravity, or death. It is a free gift of the spirit — one can accept or refuse it — & both positions are perilous. To refuse is to run the risk of dying without having lived. To accept is an even more dangerous but far more interesting possibility. A version of

Pascal's Wager — not on the immortality of the soul this time, but simply on its sheer existence.

To use religious metaphor (which we've tried so far to avoid) the millennium began five years before the end of the century, when One World came into being & banished all duality. From the Judao-Christiano-Islamic perspective however this is the false millennium of the "Anti-Christ"; which turns out not to be a "person" (except in the world of Archetypes perhaps) but an impersonal entity, a force contra naturam — entropy disguised as life. In this view the reign of iniquity must & will be challenged in the true millennium, the advent of the messiah. But the messiah is also not a single person in the world — rather, it is a collectivity in which each individuality is realized & thus (again metaphorically or imaginally) immortalized. The "people-as-messiah" do not enter into the homogenous sameness nor the infernal separation of entropic Capitalism, but into the difference & presence of revolution — the struggle, the "holy war". On this basis alone can we begin to work on a theory of reconciliation between the positive forces of religion & the cause of resistance. What we are offered here is simply the beginning of the beginning.

Dublin, Sept. 1, 1996

Note on Nationalism

Viewed as the quintessentialization of hierarchy & separation, the State can replicate itself on any level of experience — from the individual psyche to the laws of nations. And yet society can exist in theory without the State — & did so in fact for nearly a million years, 99% of the time span of the human species, thanks to the persistence of customs & institutions — and mythemes — that appear to have been designed for just this purpose, i.e. the suppression of the State & realization of the Social. War itself can be one of these institutions of "Society against the State", since (in its "primitive" form) it acts to disperse power & wealth rather than concentrate it. On another level we might say that shamanism also tends toward centrifugality of power in its emphasis on direct experience rather than mere symbolization (i.e. the shaman must "really" heal the patient, the medium must "really" be possessed, otherwise their prestige evaporates: — in some tribes shamanic failure was punishable by exile or death). The proto-State then must emerge in the moment of breakdown of centrifugal forces in war & religion. Changes in economic structure appear to follow upon this breakdown rather than cause it. [Note: The "breakdown" itself may have had economic causes but we cannot perceive them — certainly overpopulation and climatic change are inadequate "explanations"!] For instance, the replacement of hunting/gathering by agriculture failed to produce the proto-State. We cannot even blame the State on specialization of labor, since we are perfectly capable of imagining (with Fourier) a State-less Society based on fairly complex economics. The State seems almost sui generis — its birth is shrouded in a certain mystery. Something went wrong somewhere — the old myths (based on reciprocity & redistribution) collapsed before the power of a new "story" based on separation & accumulation. The precise instant is lost, although the true State lurches into archaeological view sometime around the 4th to 3rd millennium in Sumer & Egypt. In both cases the realms of war & religion seem to have coalesced to produce figurative & literal pyramid-structures impossible to conceive without tribute & slavery. The centrifugality of the social is gradually supplanted by the centripetality of power & wealth till a crisis point is reached in the catastrophic emergence of a "priest-king" & a nascent bureaucracy — the infallible signs of the true State.

The essence of the State is found in symbolization as mediation, & in mediation as alienation. These abstractions denote a brutal reality: — The appearance of History's Bootheel. Separation & expropriation must be accomplished simultaneously on both the symbolic & actual plane. Symbols must be made to do the "work" of accumulation — the State cannot expend its energy in re-creating itself in every moment. Writing for instance technologizes symbolization to the point where power can "act at a distance" — hence the "magic" of writing, its Hermetic origin — but writing itself may have been invented in order to implement an even more basic form of symbolization — i.e. money.

Let's examine the hypothesis that the State is impossible without money as symbolic exchange. Even the most primitive king (as opposed to "elder" or "chieftain") can only be defined by the creation of scarcity & the accumulation of wealth — & this double process can only be reproduced in symbolization. Generally this means that the king is somehow "sacred" & thus in himself (or herself) symbolizes the very motion of energy in or between surplus & scarcity. But this motion must be impeded if the energy-transfer can only take crude material form (actual cows or jars of wheat etc.). The essential exchange of protection-for-wealth that defines the true State must be symbolized in order to transcend what might be called the inherent egalitarianism of the material, its recalcitrance, its natural resistance to accumulation. "Protection" moreover has no overt material base, whereas wealth does — hence the State will be at a disadvantage in the exchange unless it can present its power in symbolic (non-material) form — as nothing for something.

If however the State remains impossible without money (even in its most unexpected or exotic or primitive form), money seems to be quite possible without the State. Our best evidence for this comes not only from the Past but also — so to speak — from the Future.

In the past we can discern money in the symbolic exchange & social construction of the sacrifice. When the tribe grows beyond the point where it can re-create itself in the sharing of a sacrificial animal, for instance, we might surmise that one's "due share" could be symbolized by some token. Once the "spiritual content" of these tokens is transferred to an economic sphere outside the sacrifice (as for example in the Lydian temple-coins of the 7th century BC) the existence of the tokens would then facilitate the "creation of scarcity" by symbolizing the accumulation of wealth. Thus money would precede the State. If we wish to push the origin of money even farther back into the past, we could examine the mysterious clay tokens that appeared in the Neolithic "Near East" around the 7th millennium BC, apparently as counters for commodities. Real goods that are present only in symbolic form already express the possibility of scarcity — & in fact these clay counters almost certainly stand for debt. When the symbolic counters themselves are then symbolized by writing — a concept that appears at a very precise moment datable to about 3100 BC in the city of Uruk — we can speak not only of money but of banking: the centralization of debt at the religio-political focus of power, the Temple. Thus, to put it crudely, money exists for 4000 years before it mutates into a form that makes possible the emergence of the true State.

If we look to the future — i.e. to the "logic" of the present — we can see even more clearly that money exists beyond the State. In a situation where money is "free" to move across borders in defiance of all political economy, as in "neo-liberal" free-market internationalism, the State can find itself abandoned by money, & re-defined as a zone of scarcity rather than wealth. The State remains by definition mired in production, while money attains the transcendence of pure symbolization. In the last five years money has achieved almost absolute lift-off, since more than 90% of all money now refers to nothing in the sphere of production, not even to the dirty outmoded symbolic tokens called "cash" — although the entire productive world remains utterly in the power of money, such that scarcely a tomato can be grown & eaten without the mediation of symbolic exchange.

Paracelsus once told a petty German king, "Your Majesty is the true alchemist, not me (a mere puffer)! Your Majesty has only to empower a bank with a monopoly to coin money, and then borrow it. Thus you will create something out of nothing, a far more puissant act than making lead into gold!" The joke here is that the king was not the real alchemist. The locus of the magical act lay in the bank not the court. When all thrones in the world were hopelessly in debt to their own self-created central banks, the focus of power shifted. When governments resign their ancient role of protection, money breaks free at last — governments can now provide only nothing for nothing — their power is shattered. Their power has migrated into the alchemical sphere of pure symbolization.

Thus money & the State have never — at any point — been exactly identical, or even necessarily in alliance. Like the paradoxical relation of money & religion, money & the State are sometimes in conspiracy, sometimes in competition, occasionally even at war. God & Moloch, Mammon & Moloch — the intricacies of their cosmic dance might be revealed in the legend of the Templars — or the IMF! Money & the State (& religion) do not possess the simple paradoxicality of the ancient riddle about chicken & egg, but a far more complex relation; the question about cause & effect is the wrong question.

Money, the State, & religion: — all are powers of oppression, but not the same power of oppression. In fact, when deployed against each other, they can act as powers of liberation. Money "buys freedom" for example; the populist State can suppress the banks, thus freeing its citizens from "money-power"; and religion has been known to deploy its "higher morality" against both economic & political injustice.

Moreover, the State does not appear all at once in its "absolute" form. If "primitive" societies possess institutions which successfully prevent the emergence of the State, nevertheless the emergence of the State cannot erase these institutions all at once. The "early" State must still co-exist with "customs & rights" that enable Society to resist its power. In ancient Ireland for example the kingship had to depend on (and often contend with) semi-independent warrior bands, the fianna, whose lives were devoted to sources of power (raiding) and wealth (hunting) that remained essentially outside the control of the State. The anthropology of "Society against the State" can be extended to a sociology of historical State systems (such as "feudalism") where some potent institutions & mythemes work against the total accumulation of power — usually at the cost of violence. Moreover, as Karl Polyani noted, money is also held in check in "pre-modern" cultures, not just in "primitive" societies (where money simply fails to appear), but also in quite complex State systems. "Classical civilizations" such as Mesopotamia, Greece, Mesoamerica, Egypt & even Rome remained structures of redistribution of wealth to some extent — if only as panem et circenses; no one could have conceived of a "free" market in such circumstances, since its obvious inhumanity would have violated every surviving principle of reciprocity — not to mention religious law. It was left to our glorious modern era to conceive of the State as absolute power, & money as "free" of all social restraint. The result might be called the Capital State: the power of money wedded to the power of war. Ultimately, once the struggle against Communism was won, it would be logical to expect a last & final struggle between Capital & the State for power pure & supreme. Instead the Molochian State appears to know that it was already secretly beaten long ago (all thrones hopelessly in debt...) & has capitulated without a whimper to the triumph of Mammon. With a few exceptions the nations are now falling all over themselves in their eagerness to "privatize" everything from health to prisons to air & water to consciousness itself. "Protection" — the only real excuse for the State's existence — evaporates in every sphere of government's influence, from tariffs to "human rights". The State seems somehow to believe it can renounce not only its vestigial power over money but even its basic functions, & yet survive as an elected occupying army! Even the US, which boasts of itself as the last & final "superpower", found itself in the very moment of its apocalyptic victory reduced to a mercenary force at the bidding of international Capital — blustering bush-league bully boasting of its crusade to overthrow a "Hitler" of the Middle East, but capable only of serving the interests of oil cartels & banks. National borders must survive so that political hirelings can divert taxes to "corporate welfare"; & so that huge profits can be made on arbitrage & currency exchange; & so that labor can be disciplined by "migratory" capital. Otherwise the State retains no real function — everything else is empty ceremony, & the sheer terrorism of the "war on crime" (i.e. the State's post-Spectacular war on its own poor and different). Thatcher & Reagan foretold with true prescience what government should & would do once it had fulfilled its last historical goal — the overthrow of the Evil Empire. Government would voluntarily dismantle itself (at the "people's" bidding of course) & gracefully submit to the real Hegelian absolute: — money.

Of course to speak of the "end of History" when there has been no ending (for example) of writing — nor for that matter of material production — is merely a form of insanity — perhaps even a terminal form! Like religion, the State has simply failed to "go away" — in fact, in a bizarre extension of the thesis of "Society against the State", we can even re-imagine the State as an institutional type of "custom & right" which Society can wield (paradoxically) against an even more "final" shape of power — that of "pure Capitalism". This is an uncomfortable thought for a good anarchist; we've always tended to view the State as the enemy, & capitalism as one of its aspects or "accidents". The ideal opposite of the anarch is the monarch. [In fact there were some amusing & futile attempts in fin-de-siècle France to forge links between anarchism & monarchism against the common enemy, the fading illusion of "democracy" — & the emerging reality of Capitalism.] In this sense we may have been outthought by syndicalism & by "council-communism", which at least developed more mature economic critiques of power. Like the left in general however anarchism collapsed in 1989 (a growing North-american movement for example suddenly imploded) in all likelihood because at that moment our enemy the State also secretly collapsed. In order to move into the gap left by the defeat of Communism we needed a critique of Capitalism as the single power in a unified world. Our careful & sophisticated critique of a world divided into two forms of State/economic power was rendered suddenly irrelevant. In an attempt to rectify this lack, I believe we need a new theory of "nationalism" as well as a new theory of Capitalism (and indeed a new theory of religion as well). So far the only interesting model for this is the EZLN in Mexico — (it's gratifying to see Zapatista slogans scrawled all over Dublin!) — & it would be worth analyzing their theory-&-praxis for inspiration. The EZLN is the first revolutionary force to define itself in opposition to "global neo-liberalism"; it has done so without aid or influence from the "Internationale" because it appeared in the very same moment that "Moscow" disappeared. It has received the support of the remnants of Liberation Theology as well as the secret councils of Mayan shamans & traditional elders. In the Native-american sense of the word it is a "nationalist" movement, & yet it derives its political inspiration from Zapata, Villa, & Flores Magon (i.e., two agrarian anarcho-syndicalists & one anarcho-communist). It is concerned with "empirical freedoms" rather than purist ideology. [As Qaddafi says, "In need, freedom remains latent".] No wonder the *NYTimes* called Chiapas the first "post-modern" revolution; in fact, it is the first revolution of the 21st century.

James Connolly, one of the founders of the IWW, developed in Ireland a theory that socialism & nationalism were parts of one & the same cause — & for this theory he suffered martyrdom in 1916. From one point of view Connolly's theory might lead toward "National Socialism" on the Right — but from another point of view it leads to "third world nationalism" on the Left. Now that both these movements are dead it is possible to see more clearly how Connolly's theory also fits with anarchist & syndicalist ideas of his own period, such as the left volkism of Gustav Landauer or the "General Strike" of Sorel. These ideas in turn can be traced back to Proudhon's writings on mutualism & "anarcho-federalism". [The quarrel between Marx & Proudhon was far more unfortunate for history than Marx's much noisier & more famous quarrel with Bakunin.] Inasmuch as we might propose a "neo-proudhonian" interpretation of the Zapatista uprising, therefore, Connolly's ideas may take on a new relevance for us [and thus perhaps it's not surprising if the EZLN sparks a response from the Irish left!]. Nationalism today is headed for a collision with Capitalism, for the simple reason that the nation per se has been redefined by Capital as a zone of depletion. In other words, the nation can either capitulate to Capitalism or else resist it — no third way, no "neutrality" remains possible. The question facing the nation as zone of resistance is whether to launch its revolt from the Right (as "hegemonic particularity") or from the left (as "non-hegemonic particularity"). Not all nations are zones of resistance, & not all zones of resistance are nations. But wherever the two coincide to some extent the choice becomes not only an ethical but also a political process.

During the American Civil War the anarchist Lysander Spooner refused to support either side — the South because it was guilty of chattel-slavery, the North because it was guilty of wage-slavery — & moreover because it denied the right to secede, an obvious sine qua non of any genuinely free federation. In this sense of the term, nationalism must always be opposed because it is hegemonic — & secession must always be supported inasmuch as it is anti-hegemonic. That is, it can only be supported to the extent that it does not seek power at the expense of others' misery. No State can ever achieve this ideal — but some "national struggles" can be considered objectively revolutionary provided they meet basic minimal requirements — i.e. that they be both non-hegemonic & anti-Capitalist. In the "New World" such movements might perhaps include the Hawaiian secession movement, Puerto Rican independence, maximum autonomy for Native-american "nations", the EZLN, & at least in theory the bioregionalist movement in the US — and it would probably exclude (with some regrets) such movements as Quebec nationalism, & the militia movement in the US. In Eastern Europe we might see potential in such states as Slovenia, Bosnia, Macedonia, the Ukraine — but not in Serbia nor in Russia. In the "Mid-East" one cannot help supporting Chechnya & the Kurds. In West Europe the EU must be opposed, & the smaller nations most likely to be crushed by the weight of Eurotrash & Eurodollars should be encouraged to stay out of the Union or to oppose it from within. This includes the Atlantic littoral from Morocco (where Berber resistance & Saharan independence have our sympathy) to Ireland, Denmark, perhaps Scandanavia, the Baltics, & Finland. Celtic secessionism should be encouraged in Scotland, Wales, Brittany, & Man; this would add a strong socialist & green tint to any possible coalition of small Atlantic States. In Northern Ireland the best possible solution to the "Troubles" might be an independent Ulster based on socialist anti-sectarian solidarity — a dream perhaps but far more interesting than "Peace" at any price — & a free revolutionary Ulster would no doubt release an unbelievable burst of energy into the anti-Capitalist movement — despite its size Ulster would emerge as a leader of any such movement — it would possess tremendous moral prestige.

Since we're indulging in dreams let's imagine that an anti-Communist/anti-Capitalist movement emerges in E. Europe, & allies itself with new movements within Islam, no longer "fundamentalist" & hegemonistic but definitely anti-Capitalist & opposed to "One World" culture. In turn an alliance is made with the anti-capitalist anti-"Europe" states of the Atlantic littoral — & simultaneously within all these countries revolutionary forces are at work for social & economic justice, environmental activism, anti-hegemonic solidarity, & "revolutionary difference". NGOs & religious groups lend their logistical support to the struggle. Meanwhile we can imagine Capitalism in crisis for any of a myriad reasons, from bank-collapse to environmental catastrophe. Suddenly the radical populist critique of "neo-liberalism" begins to cohere for millions of workers, farmers, tribal peoples, x-class drop-outs & artists, heretics, & even "petit-bourgeois" shopkeepers & professionals...

..."After the Revolution" of course all nationalist forms would have to be carefully reconsidered. The goal of "neo-Proudhonian federalism" would be the recognition of freedom at every point of organization in the rhizome, no matter how small — even to a single individual, or any tiny group of "secessionists". No doubt these freedoms would have to be ensured through constant struggle against the "natural" tendencies to greed & power-hunger inherent within every individual & every collectivity. But that's a matter for the future. In the present we are faced with the monumental task of constructing an anti-Capitalist resistance movement out of the shattered remnants of radicalism, some glue, some tissue paper, & some hot rhetoric. We can no longer afford the luxury of ignoring politics. This does not mean I'm about to ruin a perfect anarchist record & vote for the first time — since in my country voting means nothing & gains one nothing, not even $5 or a free drink (as in the old days of Tammany Hall). I mean politics in the Clauswitzian sense. And war makes for strange bedfellows — even for unexpected comrades & allies. I'd like to believe that revolution could be a non-violent "war for peace" — but like a good scout, one should be prepared.

Dublin, Sept. 23, 1996

◆ More Autonomedia / Semiotext(e) titles ◆

▲ AUTONOMEDIA NEW AUTONOMY SERIES ▲
JIM FLEMING & PETER LAMBORN WILSON, EDITORS

Friendly Fire
Bob Black

Caliban and the Witches
Silvia Federici

X Texts
Derek Pell

TAZ: The Temporary Autonomous Zone,
Ontological Anarchy, Poetic Terrorism
Hakim Bey

This Is Your Final Warning!
Thom Metzger

First and Last Emperors:
The Absolute State & the Body of the Despot
Kenneth Dean & Brian Massumi

Warcraft
Jonathan Leake

This World We Must Leave and Other Essays
Jacques Camatte

Spectacular Times
Larry Law

Future Primitive and Other Essays
John Zerzan

Wiggling Wishbone
Stories of Patasexual Speculation
Bart Plantenga

The Electronic Disturbance
Critical Art Ensemble

♦ More Autonomedia / Semiotext(e) Titles ♦

Invisible Governance
The Art of African Micropolitics
David Hecht & Maliqalim Simone

Cracking the Movement
Squatting Beyond the Media
Foundation for the Advancement of Illegal Knowledge

The Lizard Club
Steve Abbott

Whore Carnival
Shannon Bell, ed.

Crimes of Culture
Richard Kostelanetz

Capital and Community
Jacques Camatte

The Root Is Man
Dwight Macdonald

Carnival of Chaos
Sascha Altman Debrul

Pirate Utopias
Moorish Corsairs & European Renegadoes
Peter Lamborn Wilson

Shower of Stars
The Dream & the Book
Peter Lamborn Wilson

Millennium
Hakim Bey

Electronic Civil Disobedience
Critical Art Ensemble

Beyond Bookchin
David Watson

◆ More Autonomedia / Semiotext(e) titles ◆

▲ SEMIOTEXT(E) DOUBLE AGENTS SERIES ▲
Jim Fleming & Sylvère Lotringer, Editors

Fatal Strategies
Jean Baudrillard

Foucault Live
Collected Interviews of Michel Foucault
Michel Foucault

Archeology of Violence
Pierre Clastres

Lost Dimension
Paul Virilio

Aesthetics of Disappearance
Paul Virilio

Collected Interviews of William S. Burroughs
William S. Burroughs

▲ SEMIOTEXT(E), THE JOURNAL ▲
Jim Fleming & Sylvère Lotringer, Editors

Polysexuality
François Peraldi, ed.

Semiotext(e) USA
Jim Fleming & Peter Lamborn Wilson, eds.

Oasis
Timothy Maliqalim Simone, et al., eds.

Semiotext(e) SF
Rudy Rucker, Robert Anton Wilson, Peter Lamborn Wilson, eds

Semiotext(e) Architecture
Hraztan Zeitlian, ed.

Radiotext(e)
Neil Strauss & Dave Mandl, eds.

Semiotext(e) Canadas
Jordan Zinovich, ed.

◆ More Autonomedia / Semiotext(e) titles ◆

▲ SEMIOTEXT(E) FOREIGN AGENTS SERIES ▲
Jim Fleming & Sylvère Lotringer, Editors

POPULAR DEFENSE & ECOLOGICAL STRUGGLES
Paul Virilio

SIMULATIONS
Jean Baudrillard

GERMANIA
Heiner Müller

COMMUNISTS LIKE US
Félix Guattari & Toni Negri

ECSTASY OF COMMUNICATION
Jean Baudrillard

IN THE SHADOW OF THE SILENT MAJORITIES
Jean Baudrillard

FORGET FOUCAULT
Jean Baudrillard

REMARKS ON MARX
Michel Foucault

STILL BLACK, STILL STRONG
Dhoruba Bin Wahad, Mumia Abu-Jamal & Assata Shakur

SADNESS AT LEAVING
Erje Ayden

LOOKING BACK ON THE END OF THE WORLD
Jean Baudrillard, Paul Virilio, et al.

NOMADOLOGY: THE WAR MACHINE
Gilles Deleuze & Félix Guattari

PURE WAR
Paul Virilio & Sylvère Lotringer

METATRON
Sol Yurick

More Autonomedia / Semiotext(e) Titles

Bolo'bolo
P.M.

On the Line
Gilles Deleuze & Félix Guattari

Speed and Politics
Paul Virilio

Driftworks
Jean-François Lyotard

69 Ways to Play the Blues
Jürg Laederach

Inside & Out of Byzantium
Nina Zivancevic

Assassination Rhapsody
Derek Pell

Chaosophy
Félix Guattari

The Politics of Truth
Michel Foucault

Soft Subversions
Félix Guattari

Semiotext(e) Native Agents Series
Chris Kraus, Editor

If You're A Girl
Ann Rower

Not Me
Eileen Myles

**Walking through Clear Water
In a Pool Painted Black**
Cookie Mueller

◆ MORE AUTONOMEDIA / SEMIOTEXT(E) TITLES ◆

HANNIBAL LECTER, MY FATHER
Kathy Acker

SICK BURN CUT
Deran Ludd

THE MADAME REALISM COMPLEX
Lynne Tillman

HOW I BECAME ONE OF THE INVISIBLE
David Rattray

THE ORIGIN OF *THE* SPECIES
Barbara Barg

I LOVE DICK
Chris Kraus

THE NEW FUCK YOU
ADVENTURES IN LESBIAN READING
Eileen Myles & Liz Kotz, eds.

READING BROOKE SHIELDS
THE GARDEN OF FAILURE
Eldon Garnet

▲ AUTONOMEDIA BOOK SERIES ▲

SOUNDING OFF!
MUSIC AS SUBVERSION/ RESISTANCE/REVOLUTION
Ron Sakolsky & Fred Wei-Han Ho

UNBEARABLES
The Unbearables

THE DAUGHTER
Roberta Allen

FILE UNDER POPULAR
THEORETICAL & CRITICAL WRITINGS ON MUSIC
Chris Cutler

More Autonomedia / Semiotext(e) Titles

Magpie Reveries
James Koehnline

On Anarchy & Schizoanalysis
Rolando Perez

God & Plastic Surgery
Marx, Nietzsche, Freud & the Obvious
Jeremy Barris

Marx Beyond Marx
Lessons on the Gründrisse
Antonio Negri

Rethinking Marxism
Steve Resnick & Rick Wolff, eds.

The Touch
Michael Brownstein

Gulliver
Michael Ryan

Model Children
Inside the Republic of Red Scarves
Paul Thorez

Scandal: Essays in Islamic Heresy
Peter Lamborn Wilson

The Arcane of Reproduction
Housework, Prostitution, Labor & Capital
Leopoldina Fortunati

Clipped Coins, Abused Words, Civil Government
John Locke's Philosophy of Money
Constantine George Caffentzis

Trotskyism and Maoism
Theory & Practice in France & the U.S.
A. Belden Fields

Film & Politics in the Third World
John Downing, ed.

More Autonomedia / Semiotext(e) Titles

Columbus & Other Cannibals
The Wétiko Disease & The White Man
Jack Forbes

Enragés & Situationists in the Occupation Movement, May '68
René Viénet

Cassette Mythos
The New Music Underground
Robin James, ed.

Xerox Pirates
"High" Tech & the New Collage Underground
Autonomedia Collective, eds.

The Narrative Body
Eldon Garnet

Popular Reality
Irreverend David Crowbar, ed.

Zerowork
The Anti-Work Anthology
Bob Black & Tad Kepley, eds.

The New Enclosures
Midnight Notes Collective

Midnight Oil
Work, Energy, War, 1973–1992
Midnight Notes Collective

A Day in the Life
Tales from the Lower East Side
Alan Moore & Josh Gosniak, eds.

Gone to Croatan
Origins of North American Dropout Culture
James Koehnline & Ron Sakolsky, eds.

About Face
Race in Postmodern America
Timothy Maliqalim Simone

◆ More Autonomedia / Semiotext(e) Titles ◆

Horsexe
Essay on Transsexuality
Catherine Millot

Blood and Volts
Edison, Tesla and the Electric Chair
Th. Metzger

Format and Anxiety
Collected Essays on the Media
Paul Goodman

The Damned Universe of Charles Fort
Louis Kaplan, ed.

By Any Means Necessary
Outlaw Manifestos & Ephemera 1965–70
Peter Stansill & David Zane Mairowitz, eds.

The Official KGB Handbook
USSR Committee for State Security

Wild Children
David Mandl & Peter Lamborn Wilson., eds.

The Rotting Goddess
Classical Origins of the Witch
Jacob Rabinowitz

Dreamer of the Day
Francis Parker Yockey & the Secret Nazi International
Kevin Coogan

▲ AUTONOMEDIA DISTRIBUTION ▲

Felix
The Review of Television & Video Culture
Kathy High, ed.

Lusitania
A Journal of Reflection and Oceanography
Martim Avillez, ed.

◆ More Autonomedia / Semiotext(e) Titles ◆

Drunken Boat
An Anarchist Review of Literature & the Arts
Max Blechman, ed.

Race Traitor
A Journal of the New Abolitionism
John Garvey & Noel Ignatiev, eds.

Radio Sermonettes
The Moorish Orthodox Radio Crusade Collective
Libertarian Book Club

Aimless Wandering
Chuang Tzu's Chaos Linguistics
Hakim Bey
Xexoxial Editions

All Cotton Briefs
Expanded Edition
M. Kasper
Benzene Books

O Tribe That Loves Boys
The Poetry of Abu Nuwas
Translated and introduced by Hakim Bey
Entimos Press & The Abu Nuwas Society

▲ PLOVER PRESS ▲

The Courage to Stand Alone
Conversations with U.G. Krishnamurti
Ellen J. Chrystal & Henk Schoenville, eds.

The Mother of God
Luna Tarlo